This book is an early spring breeze through a window, just opened after a long, smoky winter. I desire every pastor, staff member, and board member in North America to read it. It is balanced, refreshing, and liberating. Glenn offers accurate biblical insight and keen practical wisdom to small churches (seventy-five people or less), and to those struggling for growth or with bureaucracy. Leaders of larger churches will also benefit greatly, as the book helps in working through a current MBA craze to get back to cooperating with God.

—Bud Hopkins
Dean and Professor Emeritus
Moody Graduate School

Pastors of small churches will find in this book a new value for, and an elevated sense of, the worth of their leadership. Dr. Daman invites small church pastors to step back from the demands and expectations of their ministry to see the task of leadership in the small church with renewed simplicity and clarity. He outlines the strengths and weaknesses of the small church, allowing pastors to see how to utilize their leadership roles to minimize the weaknesses and maximize the strengths of the small church. This book is for most pastors across North America and should become a standard work on leadership along with those of Joseph Stowell and J. Oswald Sanders.

—Vernal Wilkinson
District Representative
for Village Missions

Leading the Small Church

Leading the Small Church

HOW TO DEVELOP A TRANSFORMATIONAL MINISTRY

Glenn C. Daman

Kregel
Academic & Professional

Leading the Small Church: How to Develop a Transformational Ministry

Published by Kregel Publications, a division of Kregel, Inc., P.O. Box 2607, Grand Rapids, MI 49501.

Library of Congress Cataloging-in-Publication Data
Daman, Glenn.
Leading the small church: how to develop a transformational ministry / by Glenn Daman.
p. cm.
Includes bibliographical references.
1. Small churches. 2. Pastoral theology. I. Title.
BV637.8.D35 2006
253—dc22 2006008678
CIP

ISBN 0-8254-2447-X

Printed in the United States of America

06 07 08 09 10 / 5 4 3 2 1

To my uncle, Edward Goodrick, whose passion for the small church was only surpassed by his passion for Greek. His teaching at Multnomah School of the Bible demonstrated a passion, too, for the biblical text, and his godly life was a constant model of what it means to be a true follower of Christ. He was one who truly "preached the word" and "set an example for the believers."

To the people of Tensed Community Church in Tensed, Idaho, many of whom are now present with the Lord, whose legacy remains because they taught a young man from the pages of Scripture and provided an example of what it means to walk in obedience to Christ. Their names—Wayne and Ruth Daman, Lewis and Bernice Tanner, Ole and Lola Flolo, George and Francis Dohrman, Stu and Marlene Dohrman, Vern and Kay Mitchell, Bill and Ruthie Rosenberry, Ed and Marie Berreth, Myron Johnson, Pastor Dave and Donna Gomitz, and Pastor Eric and Rogene Fisher—may not be written in the pages of church history, but they are written in the Book of Life.

Contents

Foreword

North American churches today need Jesus, to abide in Him as branches do the vine, to bear His fruit. In a time when churches are heavy laden with tradition, corporate management, liturgy, legalism, or death, Dr. Glenn Daman's book helps us to "dress down," like young David removing Saul's armor, to find freedom, life, and hope.

During the 1950s, conservative churches began to discover a new way to lead congregations—different from the top down, pastor-autocratic style—by incorporating ideas from educated members. This church "boomer" movement corresponded with reforms taking place in the corporate world, where leadership styles were becoming less authoritarian and more open and collegial. Over the past fifty years, church leaders have been in a sometimes vicious race to discover the secrets of growth and success. Even today, pastors nationwide attend seminars, read books, and correspond with one another, trying to nail down how to build and sustain the "megachurch."

As congregations have sought to move from small to big, however, few assessments have been published of the unfortunate church disasters along the way. For some, total contact with the Bible has been lost. Sunday morning has become no different from any weekday morning.

If God is indeed alive and present in the church today, as the New Testament claims, how does He intend for the church to function? Jesus said that He would build His church. If so, how does He do it? How do we, as church leaders, attain the balance between God's initiative and our cooperation? Does God still use people as He did in the writing (inspiration) of the Bible, or as He does in the illumination and proclamation of the Bible? Is it possible to accomplish God's desire for the church by using identical techniques to those employed in the secular business world?

If the church is the body of Christ, and Christ works through its members, how do we achieve a life and ministry where the body of believers is in perfect harmony with the Head and with each other, without overloading the church with efforts and programs that burden and grieve the Holy Spirit? Conversely, how do we avoid the opposite extreme, where the church is largely inactive, passively waiting for God to pull the puppet strings and cause ministry to happen?

To succeed, we must have *vision* (an agreed-upon destination); *objectives* (commonly understood goals that we attempt to achieve); and a *plan* (a road map to establish and maintain unity and order). But should the leaders of the church merely declare these essentials ex cathedra, or should they be introduced gradually as the church develops, as in the care and nurture of a growing child, timed to coordinate with its growth? Do we not introduce our children to the disciplines and routines of life as they grow, rather than forcing them into those forms all at once? If the external signs of exercise and behavior are expressions of the internal life of the church, it seems that the methodologies and forms of church life should follow a path of development and flow out of the natural life of the church.

Dr. Glenn Daman, a seasoned small-church pastor of many years, as well as an able theologian and effective practitioner, navigates with wisdom and grace the troubled waters of church growth and leadership. Dr. Daman, who now serves as an educator and consultant in leadership training, artfully explains the mystery of church life, how Christ came not to program people from the outside in but to transform individuals, the church, and even the community from the inside out—all in a manner that modern management principles cannot duplicate. For God's servants, the author's discussions of character, preaching, administration, and relationships return excitement and joy to these old, well-worn elements, for they are venues through which Christ expresses His life and power.

This book is logically structured so that readers may follow the biblical progression of Dr. Daman's thought, see the beautiful unity and order of God's plan for achieving concord and strength in the church, and avoid the hazards of making God's people into an institution or sensationalizing His message. Glenn Daman is a master of explaining the many metaphors used in Scripture—such as shepherd, family, body, vine, flock, field (crop), and wind—and how they translate into practical church ministry today.

—BUD HOPKINS
Dean and Professor Emeritus
Moody Graduate School

INTRODUCTION

The Call to Shepherds

> I am the good shepherd. The good shepherd lays down his life for the sheep. The hired hand is not the shepherd who owns the sheep. So when he sees the wolf coming, he abandons the sheep and runs away. Then the wolf attacks the flock and scatters it. The man runs away because he is a hired hand and cares nothing for the sheep. I am the good shepherd; I know my sheep and my sheep know me—just as the Father knows me and I know the Father—and I lay down my life for the sheep. (John 10:11–15)

> Be shepherds of God's flock that is under your care, serving as overseers—not because you must, but because you are willing, as God wants you to be; not greedy for money, but eager to serve; not lording it over those entrusted to you, but being examples to the flock. And when the Chief Shepherd appears, you will receive the crown of glory that will never fade away. (1 Peter 5:2–4)

The purpose of this book is to call pastors back to a shepherding ministry. In this age of "bigger is better," and a preoccupation with success, many of us have lost sight of our original calling. We are not called to build grand buildings. We are not called to run efficient organizations that remain on the cutting edge. We are not called to market the church. Instead, we are appointed to serve as undershepherds of God's flock, following the pattern and instruction of the Good Shepherd, who takes personal responsibility for the health and growth of the Lord's flock. Although there is much we pastors can learn about efficiency, marketing, and strategy from the church-growth movement, we must never allow those things to distract us from our primary calling.

This book begins by exploring what it means to be a shepherd of God's flock. The intent is not to give a comprehensive assessment of the task, or offer all the solutions. In some respects, more questions are raised than answered. In no way should the contents be interpreted as criticizing pastors who serve in large churches, or their programs and organizations. For those of us (including me) who serve in small churches, there is much we can and should learn from pastors of large churches and the strategies they have developed. Nor do the contents of this book imply that small churches are necessarily better. Many pastors who serve large churches have been and continue to be true shepherds—not only of their own congregations but of the broader church as well. Likewise, many pastors who serve in small churches have become as hired hands, bent on their own success and career advancement rather than on the care and nurture of their congregations.

This book is meant to serve as a corrective challenge, an appeal to reexamine the task to which we are called and to reassess how we measure success in ministry. Its purpose is to summon pastors of small churches back to the simplicity of ministry, to reestablish the importance of caring for the flocks we serve by loving the people we serve; proclaiming God's Word in a relevant, life-changing way; and setting a godly example. It is hoped that this book provides helpful counsel for those who serve in small churches, so that they might stand at the end of their ministry—knowing that they have fought the good fight, have finished the race, have kept the faith, and that there is in store a crown of righteousness which the Lord, the righteous Judge, will award on that day to all who have longed for his appearing (see 2 Tim. 4:7–8).

ONE

Returning to an Old Paradigm

What is pastoral leadership? What is the pastor's role in the church? What determines a successful pastor? Nothing is more fundamental and critical to the health of the church than our answers to these questions. Yet, for all that is written today about church leadership, the pastor's call and responsibility remain points of contention among students of the church and points of confusion among the laity of the church. The reason both groups struggle in attempting to answer these questions is because the church is viewed through several lenses (fig. 1.1). The first lens is that of Scripture.

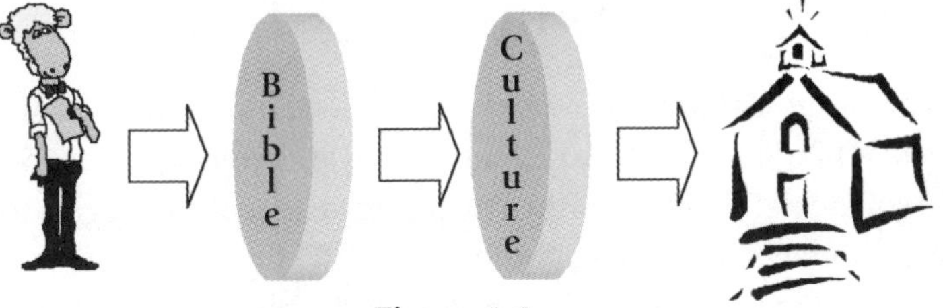

Figure 1.1.

This biblical lens is the one that should be kept clear and free from distortion and confusion. It is also the one that is normative for every church in every age. It defines church leadership and how leaders are to function within the church.

The second lens is the cultural lens, which is often determined by a congregation's specific setting and personal presuppositions regarding the church. The cultural lens of a small church differs radically from the cultural lens of a larger congregation. This lens is never free from distortion or confusion, because personal views often influence how people understand the church.

In an ideal world, the two lenses would be placed together in series so that the biblical lens would dictate and govern the parameters by which the church is seen and understood through the cultural lens.

As believers, however, we live in a fallen world, where cultural expectations and biases often cloud human perspective, the two lenses often merge into one. Now, instead of the church being seen through separate biblical and cultural lenses, it is almost impossible to distinguish what is biblical in view and what is cultural (fig. 1.2).

Figure 1.2.

The result is that the church is often viewed from a cultural perspective that is assumed to be also biblical. No longer does Scripture set the parameters for the culture; instead, culture begins to set the parameters for understanding Scripture. In this reversal of priorities, the lens of culture comes first and distorts the understanding of the biblical model of the church (fig. 1.3).

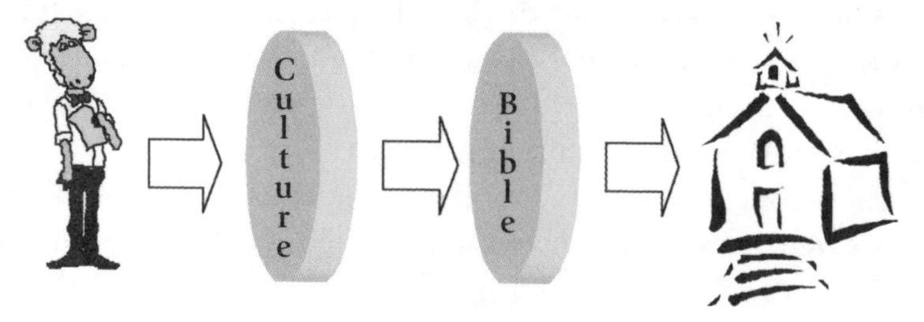

Figure 1.3.

This distortion has often occurred in the contemporary development of a church theology. Church ministry is now viewed through the lens of the business world, developing biblical support for a ministry based on corporate and commercial ideas. Terms and concepts of leadership are no longer derived from Scripture; instead they are adapted from successful businesses. A comparison of recent books written for secular leaders and books written for church leaders yields little difference in content. The leadership paradigms in the secular community and in the church often reflect the same underlying perspectives. The only difference is that many in the church try to give biblical support to these secular principles, often through prooftexting rather than sound exegesis.

The problem with allowing cultural norms to define theology is that polls and trends begin to supplant scriptural definitions of ministry and the church. When culture defines the theology of the church, the question is no longer, "Is it biblical?" Rather, the questions has become, "Is it *relevant* and *practical?*" Jesus, however, in preparing his disciples for leadership, drew a sharp distinction between biblical and secular leadership. This difference is not peripheral—that is, dealing only with the application of principles; it is essential, penetrating to the very core of the way leadership is understood, and affecting both purpose and process. In contrasting the two paradigms of leadership, Christ pointed out that secular leadership emphasizes authority and power, whereas the biblical paradigm focuses on service and humility (Matt. 20:24–28; Luke 22:24–27). The biblical paradigm focuses on proclamation, transformation, and service rather than on vision, goals, direction, management, or authority. Biblical leaders are first and foremost shepherds who care for the spiritual needs of the people. Spiritual leadership focuses on joyful service and spiritual growth rather than personal gain and success (2 Cor. 1:24; 1 Peter 5:2–3). This is not to say that vision, goals, and effective management are unimportant to the church and its pastoral leadership. They are important—but they are secondary to the primary tasks of preaching, mentoring, and providing spiritual care.

The New Paradigm for Leadership

The rise of the industrial age brought with it new models of leadership that transformed our culture and radically affected our definitions and expectations of leadership. The leadership methodologies that for generations had enabled people to run their family farms and small businesses were completely inadequate for operating an industrial enterprise. Terminology that was never heard of in the agricultural community began to appear in the culture of big business. Goals, vision, management, efficiency, effectiveness, and methodology became the new catchwords and concepts.

This rapidly evolving new paradigm of leadership significantly affected the way pastors view the church. Instead of the traditional idea of the church as a parish or a community, we now began to see it as an organization to run. The pastor's role, which had long been seen as a vocation—a calling to shepherd the flock and proclaim the truth—now became a *profession* responsible for keeping the organizational structure of the church moving forward efficiently, effectively, proactively. As David Wells points out in *No Place for Truth,* "In this new clerical order, technical and managerial competence in the church have plainly come to dominate the definition of pastoral services. It is true that matters of spirituality loom large in the churches, but it is not at all clear that churches expect the pastor to do anything more than to be a good friend. The older role of the pastor as broker of truth has been eclipsed by the newer managerial functions."[1]

The Church as an Organizational Institution

In this new industrial/corporate paradigm, organization informed the practical understanding of how the church was to function, even though the theological definition of the church hadn't changed. Within the emerging model, issues such as growth, market trends, and business practices—rather than a biblical model of community—became the driving forces in the church. Before long, in most congregations, the daily practices and functions of the church became organizationally determined rather than spiritually motivated. Rather than recognizing that culturally driven organizational issues have always been secondary in the church, leaders took organizational issues—such as vision casting, mission statements, program development, marketing campaigns—and made them normative. Polls and trend analysis, rather than a reliance on biblical theology and scriptural commands, began to shape church methodologies and strategies. The result is that ministry has become pragmatic in its approach, and *results*, rather than truth, define what is right.[2] The question is no longer, Is it biblically sound? but, Does it work?

In this new paradigm, Peter Drucker, Stephen Covey, Kenneth Blanchard, Warren Bennis, and other business gurus have more to say than did the theologians or the Biblicists to the contemporary church in terms of how to operate. For pastors seeking leadership counsel, it seemed at times that these individuals held more sway than the apostles Peter and Paul—or even Christ himself. It wasn't that the apostles and Christ were completely set aside, but their words were filtered through a corporate management grid established by contemporary business heroes and consultants. Ways were found to read the scriptural guidelines in light of what "worked" in the business world.

Don't misunderstand—many of the lessons learned from the business community are valuable and helpful; the mistake of the new paradigm, however, is that it seeks to make these corporate values normative for the church and essential to pastoral ministry. As a result, truth has become minimized because we don't want to offend people and drive them away, and methodology has been centralized, because we want to be effective. Many seminary pastoral programs thus place a greater emphasis on "practical theology" than on languages or biblical and systematic theology. *How* we "do church" has become more important than *what the church is.*

Instead of bringing guaranteed success to the church, however, the corporate/organizational paradigm has often left pastors feeling like the emperor in his new clothes—strutting around proclaiming the mantras of the corporate leadership model, but all the while sensing that something is terribly missing. Although pastors can learn much from the secular community, we do well to heed Paul's warning that the secular mind-set, with its priorities and values, is always to be viewed with suspicion and skepticism (1 Cor. 2:1–16; 2 Cor. 6:14–17; see also Ezek. 11:11–12). In the quest for success, we must exercise discernment and judgment before blindly following the secular paradigm. Otherwise, we risk failing to recognize that what "works" from a human perspective might not work from God's perspective. Consider, for example, Israel's initial motivation for having a king: it was the "right thing to do" from a human perspective, but resulted in spiritual bankruptcy (1 Sam. 8).

Outward organizational growth does not necessarily translate into spiritual growth. As John Piper has rightly warned, "For every incompetent pastor who justifies himself with spiritual coverings, a hundred incompetent pastors are desperately doubling their spiritual incompetence by seeking remedies in Babylon."[3] Genuine leadership manifests itself in recognizing human incompetence in light of God's sufficiency (2 Cor. 3:5–6; see also 1 Cor. 15:10; 2 Cor. 4:1; Gal. 2:7–8). We pastors (and I include myself) need to recognize that we are *all* incompetent in ministry. And further, the strategies and tactics of the business world will not ultimately overcome our weaknesses. Rather, the solution to our incompetence lies not in the paradigms of the secular business community but in a life of dependency on God. Success in ministry will never be found by shoring up our abilities and proficiencies; success in ministry can only be found by allowing God's power, grace, and character to become evident in us, and His purposes to be accomplished through us. We should remember that, in the book of Acts, preparation for ministry was *waiting* for the Holy Spirit, not taking a seminar on the latest methodology.

"Corporate structures can never produce communities," writes Glenn Wagner. "People feel used by corporations, not nurtured by them. Employees of a corporation know their sole purpose is to make someone else rich and successful, so they feel disconnected. . . . There is precious little loyalty in a corporation. Why? Because it's hard to be loyal to a machine. Could it be that's why so many people these days jump from church to church? They don't feel connected. It's hard to leave a community, but it's not tough at all to leave a corporation."[4]

The emphasis on external organizational growth has had a devastating affect on small churches and their pastors, who often view themselves as second-class citizens. Responding to the siren call of corporate success—size and numbers—and surrounded by examples of apparently successful megachurches, small-church pastors undervalue the essential biblical elements of community and relationships, and never quite feel successful. They become discouraged, wondering whether the glory of God has departed, leaving them to stagnate without any hope of experiencing God's blessing. As a result, low morale remains one of the most pervasive problems confronting small churches.

The Pastor as a Professional

Having adopted a corporate organizational mind-set, pastors now enter the ministry, viewing it as a career rather than a calling. Long-term tenures, previously the standard, have been replaced by "job hopping" as pastors move up the corporate church ladder. Small churches are seen as stepping-stones where newly graduated seminarians can gain some experience before moving on to a larger church. Small churches have become the farm teams to the major leagues of ministry. Pastors become hired guns, who come and clean up the town before moving on. Of the 221 pastors who graduated from Yale between 1745 and 1775, 71 percent stayed for the rest of their lives in the church to which they were first called, and only 4 percent had more than four pastorates. Today, the average tenure of a pastor is between two and three years.[5] As a result, small churches are finding it increasingly difficult to attract pastors who are willing to serve in a smaller church, especially those located in isolated areas.

The New Paradigm for Ministry

For the new breed of professional pastor, the ministry focus has shifted from theological proclamation to program development and organizational leadership. Pastors are no longer evaluated by the content of their sermons and the godly character revealed in their lifestyles but by their accomplishments and achievements. Accordingly, the priority of the pastor's role is to establish a vision, which is determined by assessing the community, and then building the programs and organization to fulfill that vision. The proclamation of truth often becomes secondary and is only emphasized in the pastor's preaching role. The assumption seems to be that the more successful (from a corporate-model perspective) a pastor becomes in building programs and numbers, the more spiritual that pastor is. Yet the perpetual moral failures of pastors in churches large and small reveal that numerical success and character are not necessarily related. Yet congregations will continue to follow fallen pastors because "they have done so much for the church." Character, then, plays second fiddle to achievement.

This is a far cry from the picture presented in Scripture, where character is the basis of ministry. What the writer of Proverbs says about kingdoms is equally applicable concerning the church: "When the righteous thrive, the people rejoice; when the wicked rule, the people groan" (Prov. 29:2; see also 19:10; 30:22). The security of a king was established by his character rather than the accomplishments of his armies. The same may be said of the church. It is the character of the pastor that ultimately determines the extent of that pastor's impact, not the accomplishments of that pastor's programs and methodologies. Consequently, as John Piper laments, "The professionalization of the ministry is a constant threat to the offense of the gospel. It is a threat to the profoundly spiritual nature of our work. I have seen it often: the love of professionalism (parity among the world's professionals) kills a man's belief that he is sent by God to save people from hell and to make them Christ-exalting, spiritual aliens in the world."[6]

The misconception must not be created that professionalization is only a problem for pastors of large churches; it must recognized that professionalization equally affects pastors of small churches but in a far more subtle way. We might think that because we've remained in a small church, we have not sold our birthright for the pottage of success, yet in reality we have. We judge others for serving large congregations because we're jealous of their status. We want what they have. Steve Bierly places a mirror before every pastor of a small church when he writes, "The pastor who stands behind the pulpit in [a] small church must also, of logical necessity, be very small. Sometimes I want to be big. I want articles to be written about me! I want my picture in the paper. At the very least, I'd like the church-at-large to acknowledge that I exist."[7] Pastors of small churches pursue the same remedies for the problems we face as do our colleagues in larger churches. We become methodological junkies, looking for our next procedural fix. The whole time we're running our churches as corporate businesses, albeit family-run businesses. What Eugene Peterson warns against may be evident in a church of any size: "The pastors of America have metamorphosed into a company of shopkeepers, and the shops they keep are churches. They are preoccupied with shopkeepers' concerns—how to keep the customers happy, how to lure customers away from competitors down the street, how to package the goods so that the customers will lay out more money."[8] It is no wonder that the pastorate has fallen out of favor with people entering ministry. When pastoral ministry becomes a profession, it is no longer attractive with its long hours and minimal pay. It's no surprise, then, that most small churches struggle to find people willing to come and serve, for the small church has little to offer in terms of benefit packages. When ministry becomes a job and a career rather than a calling, why would anyone go to a small church? If success in ministry is defined by program development, it makes little sense to go to a small church where there are few programs to develop.

The corporate-model approach to leadership in the church, then, remains deficient for three reasons:

1. The church has a different priority than a corporation, a fundamentally different purpose and standard of success. In a business model, the priority is on programs and methodology. In the church, the priority should be obedience to the standards of Scripture.
2. The church has a different standard of success. In the corporate model, a leader's accomplishments determine effectiveness, and results are the measure of success. In the church, a

leader's character should determine effectiveness, and that leader's ability to facilitate spiritual transformation—both individually and corporately—is the measure of success.

3. The church has a different starting point. In the corporate model, the premise is that the church is first and foremost an organization. In Scripture, however, the church is fundamentally a spiritual organism, living in connection with its head, Jesus Christ.

Inadequate Views of Success

Nowhere have cultural perspectives had a greater impact on the church than in the perception of what it takes to be a successful leader. No one enters the pastoral ministry with the view of becoming a failure. All pastors strive to attain success, and feel incredibly guilty if they come up short. Pastors of small churches often wonder whether their churches would grow if they worked harder, prayed more, were more skillful in ministry, or if their congregations were more open to new ideas. But the reason why pastors struggle in small churches and often become discouraged is not because of their work ethic or the inherent nature of small churches, or because their congregations are unwilling to change; it's because they have an inadequate view of what constitutes successful leadership. When the definition of success is incomplete or skewed, the understanding of the pastoral role becomes misguided. In considering successful church leadership, it is common to labor under several misperceptions.

Misperception 1: Successful Pastors Are Visionaries

One of the more popular perspectives of leadership today is that an effective leader is a visionary who is able to foresee what the church will become. These "visions" are not, however, necessarily derived from Scripture, but are more often based on the leader's assessment of what the church should do organizationally in relation to its setting and location and the perceived needs of the community. To many students of leadership, pastors who are not visionaries are seen as ill-equipped for ministry and likely not possessing the gift of leadership. These students lament that only 6 percent of pastors claim to have a gift of visionary leadership. But if that is true, then either the church has gone to seed and God is no longer able to equip the right people for the task of leadership, or the fault lies in the understanding of leadership and what is involved in leading the church.

Unlike many contemporary definitions of leadership, the gift of leadership mentioned in Romans 12:8 does not imply the role of setting direction for the church. That is a recent, post-industrial development. Instead, biblical leadership entails the gifts of administration and organization, which were primarily directed to the benevolent ministries of the church.[9] Further, the focus of biblical leadership is on service for the benefit of others, rather than on authority and accomplishment, as in the modern emphasis. Always in Scripture the emphasis of pastoral leadership is on the proclamation of truth and care for the flock. This is not to say that vision and direction are not important. They are. But because vision and direction are organizational issues, often determined by the prevailing culture, they are necessarily secondary in importance.

The need for visionary leadership—and its importance—may characterize the role of a pastor in a large church. It is far less important, however, for the pastor of a small church. There, relationships rather than programs provide the strength of the church, and the congregation and/or "tribal chiefs" (individuals who by their position or family relationships exert great influence over the rest of the community) run the church. Although vision is important for churches of all sizes, in a small church the vision arises from the congregation as a whole rather than from a single individual. More importantly, the pastor must have a clear understanding of the biblical vision for the church—as the body of Christ, as manifesting Christ's character, and as an avenue for transforming the people of the church to be like him.

Misperception 2: Successful Pastors Are Effective CEOs

Another common definition of a successful pastor—although a definition not as openly portrayed—is one who efficiently and effectively runs the church organization. These pastors have good management skills and are able to make decisions quickly. They have excellent time management techniques, maximizing every minute and minimizing distractions. They don't waste time on meaningless conversation or "chit-chat," but keep their focus on the task at hand. They readily delegate minor issues to others and have their administrative assistants work out all the details. They are task-oriented individuals who strive for visible, definable results.

The problem for many pastors of small churches is that an overly efficient, task-oriented approach would alienate many of the people they serve. Isolating themselves from people in order to "do the work of ministry" would be fatal to the pastor's leadership in the church. To minimize "chit-chat" would undermine one of the more important elements of their ministries—building relationships. Some of the most important shepherding is "inefficient," accomplished not in a formal teaching environment or in a scheduled counseling appointment, but over a cup of coffee, in the cab of a combine, or on a golf course, where pastors have casual opportunities to discuss real-life issues from a biblical perspective. Most of Christ's ministry occurred, in fact, not in a classroom but on thoroughfares and in town squares where he used life situations to convey spiritual truth.

Misperception 3: Successful Pastors Are Program Developers

Some people would say that successful pastors are those who have the capacity to develop, implement, and maintain effective programs and methodologies. They are constantly pushing the church to develop new strategies and programs for growing the church so that it remains on the cutting edge of ministry. They organize social programs, evangelistic events, and recovery groups. They are always sensitive to perceived needs in the church and community, and they develop the right programs in the church to match those needs.

For pastors of small churches, such an emphasis on programs and methods leads only to frustration and cynicism. It is not always that the small church is unwilling to try something new; they simply do not have the luxury of unlimited resources to develop and staff new programs. Instead, they often struggle to survive, barely maintaining existing programs. Defining successful ministries and leaders by the size of their programs creates unnecessary pressure to always be doing something newer and bigger and better.

Misperception 4: Successful Pastors Are Growth Agents

During the latter decades of the twentieth century, it was popular to say that successful pastors were those who were serving growing churches. Pastors were seen as responsible for the numerical growth of the church and for effectively leading the church through various stages of church growth. Pastors who effectively led their churches through substantial growth were lauded as successful leaders to be emulated and followed.

The reality, however, both biblically and practically, is that effective leadership does not always translate into numerical growth. Some of the greatest leaders in the Old Testament did not experience the joy of seeing substantial or even minimal growth. Elijah despaired in ministry because no one responded favorably to his victory on Mount Carmel. Isaiah, Ezekiel, and Jeremiah were called to serve people who refused to listen to their prophecies. Even Jesus, at the end of his ministry, stood alone. What has been forgotten is that the growth of the church is not the pastor's responsibility; it's God's (1 Cor. 3:7).

Misperception 5: Successful Pastors Serve Large Churches

Although it sounds unspiritual to say it, many people believe that the larger the congregation the more successful the pastor. Thus, pastors of large churches are invited to speak at conferences so that pastors of smaller churches can learn how to become more effective (i.e., build larger churches).

Although what God has accomplished through large churches should never be minimized, the lesson of the parable of the stewards is that size has, in God's eyes, nothing to do with success (Matt. 25:14–30). Nor does the size of a congregation reveal the reality of God's blessing. Instead the greatness of a church is determined by the manifest presence of God (Hag. 2:1–9). And the greatness of church leaders is determined not by their achievements but by the reality of God in their lives.

Misperception 6: Successful Pastors Are Well Loved

Another mistaken assumption is that as long as pastors are well loved and well respected, and they love the people in their congregation, then they are successful. An examination of the prophets, however, reveals that leaders often have to do and say things that make them very unpopular with the people. Although it is important for pastors to love the people in the church, and although developing positive relationships is helpful, neither of these is the measure of a pastor's success, even in a small church. Pastors can enjoy great relationships but be out of touch with what God desires to accomplish in our ministries.

The difficulty with each of these definitions of success is that there are elements of truth and validity to each of them. It is not a mistake to think they are important. Many of the principles are valid and useful in the church, even in smaller congregations. Where we as pastors go astray, however, is in thinking that they are central to an effective ministry. Although each is valuable in its own way for running a church organization, the pastor's true calling runs much deeper.

Returning to the Old Paradigm

One of the reasons for perplexity in understanding the nature of the pastor's role and what constitutes success is the failure to distinguish between the pastor as an organizational leader and the pastor as a spiritual leader.

The Pastor as an Organizational Leader

Although the church is a spiritual organism, there remains an organizational element within its structure. This organizational structure in the early church was never fully analyzed and described in Scripture, but hints of its presence can be found. Acts 6, for example, tells that the early church had social programs requiring administrative tasks. Moreover, the church had a leadership structure that included a hierarchy of authority. Elders, deacons, and deaconesses, each had different tasks and responsibilities and each possessed different degrees of authority. For one to be included in the ranks of these leaders, certain qualifications had to be met. Some passages indicate that the early church recognized official membership, although the extent of this practice is open to some debate. To become a member, individuals were required to demonstrate the genuineness of their salvation, most often through the rite of baptism (Acts 2:41, 47; 5:14). Thus, to overlook the importance of the church's organizational structure, as sometimes happens in small churches, is to overlook an important element of effective ministry. Ministry without structure becomes haphazard at best.

Clearly, the pastor, as a leader of the church, is responsible for leading the church organization. In Acts 2:45, it is found that leaders were responsible for overseeing the administration of common property. They were also responsible to see to it that everything was done in a fitting and orderly way (1 Cor. 14:40). Scripture describes and hints at the organizational nature of the church but does not prescribe a specific organizational structure or program for the church to follow. When prescriptive terms and statements are used, the focus is more often on the spiritual nature of the church and its leadership rather than on its organizational structure. To that end, the apostle Paul, in outlining the qualifications of elders, focuses on spiritual qualifications and character rather than on organizational qualifications or expertise. It is possible to have a church without, in fact, any organizational structure at all. What defines the church is not its structure, but two or more individuals meeting together for fellowship and mutual edification (Matt. 18:20).

Contrary to today's prevailing wisdom, then, the New Testament never defines a pastor's role as visionary organizational leadership. The pastor's primary responsibility is spiritual leadership. Everything else is secondary. Furthermore, the organizational structure of the church is culturally determined rather than biblically prescribed. The leaders in the early church did not follow a new, biblically mandated format; instead, they adapted the already established format of synagogue worship. And as the church expanded into Gentile communities, the organizational structure adapted accordingly. The New Testament established general organizational principles, such as the role and position of elders, but "no detailed and full-orbed organizational pattern is presented in the New Testament. Rather, the governmental structures provide basic principles of church order which may be adapted for different requirements."[10] Because today's focus is on the church as an organization, organizational issues such as vision, mission, and programs have been made normative rather than secondary in importance to the primary purpose of spiritual growth. In general, a larger church will need a more complex organizational structure than a smaller church, but in both churches this must all be kept secondary in importance to the primary task of spiritual guidance, and must remain adaptive to changing circumstances and cultural contexts.

The Pastor as a Spiritual Leader

In defining the role of a pastor, the New Testament focuses on the function of caring for the spiritual well-being of the people of God. This responsibility is primary, normative, and biblical. In the early church, when organizational duties started to supplant the apostles' spiritual role, they took immediate corrective action by establishing the role of deacon (Acts 6). In every age, spiritual leadership is prescribed as normative for all church leaders, regardless of the cultural setting, and this spiritual leadership will ultimately determine a pastor's success or failure. Consequently, it is this spiritual role that must be defined and determined biblically, not culturally. It is, after all, the original paradigm of the church, in which the focus is on the church as a spiritual organism and the visible bride of Christ, and this paradigm must remain the pastor's primary focus, regardless of all other factors.

The church is not merely an organization; it is a living organism, having all the dynamics of life itself. And as a living entity, it is supernaturally driven and governed. As a spiritual entity that has life and interdependency, the church may possess organizational attributes and characteristics, such as structure and form, but these are not what give it that life and vitality. Much of what is deemed necessary for the church as an organization—programs, plans, and formal structures—is not necessary for the church as a spiritual entity. The church can exist without organizational structure, but it cannot exist without spiritual life. In other words, the spiritual health of each individual part is interwoven with the overall health of the entire body. Pastors, then, are primarily spiritual guides who promote and maintain the spiritual health of the body of Christ. As Glenn Wagner points out, "We must come to see that the primary duties of those whom God calls to lead his church is caring for the sheep—not managing, not directing, not vision-casting, not anything else."[11]

When writing to Timothy and Titus, Paul's exhortations concerning their relational responsibilities are couched in spiritual language, with very little reference to organizational dynamics (1 Tim. 4:6–16; 2 Tim. 2:15; 4:1–9). In his challenge to the leaders of the church at Ephesus (Acts 20), Paul focuses on their spiritual roles as leaders of the church. They were to maintain close relationships with God in order to protect their own spiritual health (v. 28). They were to oversee as well the spiritual health of the congregation (v. 28). They were to be devoted to prayer by recognizing their dependency on God (v. 32), they were to center their ministry on the Scriptures (v. 32), and serve unselfishly, without seeking their own personal advantage (v. 33).

The biblical model of the pastor is not, therefore, that of an organizational CEO who effectively runs the organization by setting the vision for the church and guiding the church to growth and organizational health and prosperity. Rather, the biblical model is that of a shepherd who provides nourishment and care for the flock. The apostle Peter encourages the elders to "be shepherds of God's flock that is under your care, serving as overseers" (1 Peter 5:2). Peter is not presenting a new model he invented; he is merely passing on the model presented to him by Jesus, who challenged him to "feed my lambs" and "take care of my sheep" (John 21:15–17).

In the Old Testament, God's judgment on the leaders of Israel occurred not because of their failure to run an efficient organization, but because of their failure to shepherd God's people. In Jeremiah 12:10–11, God condemns the leaders for the spiritual apostasy of the people as well as for the leaders' lack of care and concern for the people. Instead of bringing the nation of Israel back to God

(23:1–2), they led the people astray and into idolatry (50:6). In Jeremiah 10:21, God condemns the Jewish leaders because they were not inquiring of him; instead they were pursuing their own agendas. Effective leadership begins with prayer for God's direction and for his will to be accomplished. Thus, Wagner concludes, "God makes it clear that shepherds in his service are given one overriding duty that supersedes all others: to 'bestow care on' his sheep. Not to manage them (although that must be done). Not to inspire them (although that, too, is necessary). Not even to lead them (as indispensable as that is). No. The primary concern of a shepherd in the service of the Lord should be to 'bestow care on' his sheep—and if a shepherd fails in this most fundamental of duties, God promises to 'bestow punishment' on the shepherd."[12]

The Old Paradigm

In the biblical paradigm, the single most important task of the pastor is to proclaim the truth of God's Word. As stated, preaching and teaching are never secondary to vision casting; they are always primary and central. The proclamation of truth is not, however, accomplished only from the pulpit on Sunday; proclaiming the truth is essential to all aspects of pastoral ministry. Our task as pastors is to bring Scripture to people's lives as we interact with them on a daily basis. We are to do so both publicly and privately, influencing members individually and personally so that they grow to maturity in Christ. We are not simply to organize the structure of the church; we are to transform the people who make up the church, so that they become the living body of Christ.

What the church needs today are more shepherds, not more visionaries. We need more churches in vital relationship with Jesus Christ, not bigger churches with bigger programs (or smaller churches with smaller programs). We do not need new paradigms for leadership. Instead, we must return to the ancient, biblical paradigm, the one in which pastors are spiritual caretakers of God's people, and are more concerned about the spiritual health of the congregation than about agendas, programs, and status.

The responsibility of spiritual leadership is not easy; it demands every ounce of a pastor's life and soul. Thus, as we seek to fulfill this task, we must carefully discern what is important and what is not. We need to understand clearly what marks a successful ministry, making sure that our definition of success is not determined by our culture but by the authority of Scripture. The role of the pastor is not defined by the church's organizational structure and the pastor's organizational responsibilities. Rather, because the church is the living body of Christ, spiritual in nature, it requires leaders who are first and foremost spiritual leaders who impart biblical truth to the end of transforming people toward the mind, will, and character of Christ.

TWO

Ministry

Complex or Simple?

In our quest for "success," we church leaders are in danger of over complicating pastoral ministry. Much of what has been written about ministry and leadership in the past ten years has merely led to more confusion and debate, rather than giving greater clarity to the pastoral task. Pastors are challenged to be on the cutting edge, formulating new strategies that minister to our contemporary culture, and developing new paradigms of ministry in order to remain "effective" and "relevant" in ministry. There is certainly a need for relevancy and effectiveness, but the ministerial waters often become muddied by a constant pursuit of the latest techniques, methodologies, and programs. Such a pursuit places the emphasis on effort, insight, talent, works, and perception, rather than on God's work in and through the ministry—and places pastors at risk for losing sight of the biblical simplicity of ministry.

The Danger of Overcomplicating Ministry

When we follow a business model of ministry rather than the biblical model, we lose the essential power and dynamic nature of pastoral leadership, which resides in the proclamation and application of Scripture (Rom. 1:16; Heb. 4:12–13; Titus 1:3). When our focus shifts to strategies and techniques, the goal of ministry becomes obscure and the role of pastoral leadership becomes perplexing (fig.

2.1). We end up in an endless search to find the right combination of methods and programs to make our ministry successful. Ministry becomes like a Rubik's Cube, and we are forever twisting and adjusting, hoping somehow to find the right series of steps that will enable all the pieces to fall into place, but we never quite get there.

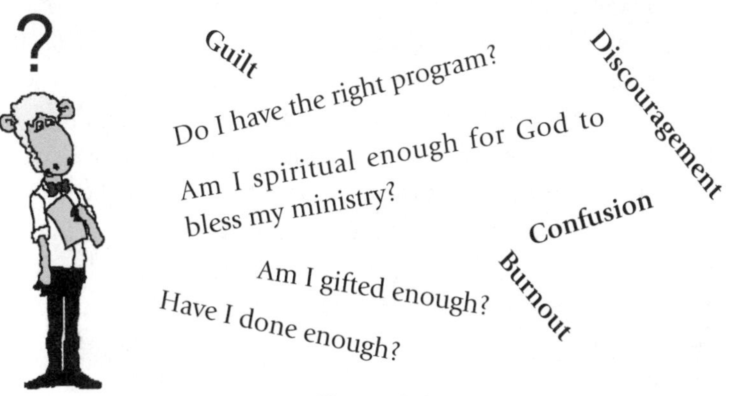

Figure 2.1.

Overcomplicating Ministry Leads to a Never-Ending Search for the Right Program

Methodology has become the new idol in the church. An idol is anything apart from God that becomes the object of our faith. In the search for success, we pastors often depend more on the rightness of our methodology than on the power and work of God's Spirit, who works through our frailties and weaknesses. Because we desire to see the church grow, it is easy as small-church pastors to become methodological junkies, always in search of a new method that will enable us to be successful in ministry. We deceive ourselves into thinking that if we could just find the right program, or the right combination of ministries, our church would be freed to grow. Consequently, we go from one seminar to another, read one book after another about "successful" churches, and implement the latest "church growth" strategy and vision. Instead of discovering the right approach, however, we leave in our wake congregations that are exhausted by trying to jump to the latest "vision" that we have for our churches. Don't get me wrong; there is a place for programs and setting a clear direction for the church. There is validity in many of the new trends, and they often do provide helpful insight into how to be relevant to the next generation. The problem arises when we begin to trust in these ideas more than in God, when we make the latest fad prescriptive for the church, or when we place the failure to adapt a new methodology on a par with disobedience to the Great Commission. Contrary to a very popular notion, our responsibility as pastors is not to "grow" the church. The responsibility for growth rests in the hands of our sovereign God (1 Cor. 3:1–9). Our responsibility is to remain faithful to our calling of proclaiming the word of God, and living as examples for others to follow (1 Tim. 4:11–16). Our responsibility is to trust God for the results and rest in the fact that he will accomplish his purposes through us. The results are *his* work—*his* success, if you will—not ours. When we place our confidence in *methods* to achieve results, we replace God with *technique.* Pastors can no more *build* the church than we can save people from their sins. Both of these tasks are the work of God in the lives of individuals and communities (Matt. 16:18; Acts 2:47; Heb. 3:3–4; 11:10). All we can do is faithfully apply God's Word to the needs and issues of our people. All we can do is point them to the Cross. Those of us who minister in small churches can derive—or ought to derive—enormous relief and freedom in this truth about our roles as pastors. It is not up to us to *grow* the church, and the size of the congregation is not indicative of our *success;* the success of the church does not depend on our wisdom, our abilities, or even our spirituality; rather, the success of the church depends on God. We are merely vessels through whom God works to accomplish his purposes. This is why *faithfulness* rather than *methodology* or *skill* is central to pastoral leadership.

Overcomplicating Ministry Leads to a Never-Ending Search for Perfect Spirituality

Because we pastors often equate success in ministry with numerical growth, and numerical growth with God's pleasure, we attribute our lack of success to a lack of spirituality. If only we were more perfect—or so we reason—our ministries would be more effective. Our churches have remained small—or so we tacitly believe—because we do not pray enough, visit enough, read the Bible (or other books) enough, or else we have too much sin in our lives. The result is a constant sense of guilt. That sense of guilt is, however, a false guilt, because we will never be perfect in this lifetime. No matter how good we might become, there is a sense in which we are never good enough: we all still sin. Even the apostle Paul confessed a painful awareness of his own sinfulness (1 Tim. 1:16). The longer we are in ministry, the more we realize our own sinful inadequacies. The problem, however, is not in our inadequacies; it's that we don't allow our inadequacies to drive us to God in complete dependency and in search of his grace. Instead, we become guilt ridden and discouraged, attributing our churches' lack of growth to our failure to live in full obedience. As Steve Bierly points out, "Small-churchaholics . . . are addicted to feeling guilty."[1] Whenever good things fail to happen—or worse, when bad things happen—we pastors see it as another example of our sins making us like Achan in the camp (Josh. 7). Perhaps the greatest stress faced in ministry is not the stress of our schedules, or the stress of "dealing with people's burdens," but rather the stress of our own humanity. We are all still sinners and painfully aware of our plight. Furthermore, the enemy knows where to attack us. There are times when people question our integrity and point out our faults—sometimes lovingly, with the desire to help us grow; more often critically, in order to elevate themselves and their agendas. When this happens, our spiritual insecurities rise to the surface and we question our fitness to be pastors.

Even when things are going well, we still feel the pain of our sinfulness. Perhaps even more discouraging than having our weaknesses pointed out are those times when people begin to elevate us onto "supersaint" pedestals. The more they venerate us, the greater our sense of guilt: "If they only knew what was truly in my heart." So we end up endlessly chasing perfection, all the while dodging criticism or living a lie of superspirituality that destroys our authenticity in ministry. In the end, we either become overwhelmed by our guilt or we deny our own frailty and weaknesses, even to ourselves.

In either case, we are robbed of the joy of ministry and become susceptible to spiritual and emotional burnout.

It isn't that spirituality and maturity are not important in ministry. We do, after all, minister from the context of character, and we lead spiritually by modeling consistent, godly lifestyles. We must also recognize, however, that we are still imperfect. We are going to fail. None of us deserves anything from God, and we are not worthy of God's blessing, even in the ministry. But our spiritual shortcomings shouldn't cause us to become discouraged in ministry; they should cause us to be authentic. Humility and authenticity come when we realize that we are no better than anyone else and we are on the pilgrimage to spiritual maturity along with the people we serve. Our being pastors does not make us exempt from the struggles that accompany the spiritual life. We will be stronger leaders when we realize our own vulnerability to sin and our need for God's continual grace and forgiveness. This awareness of our sinfulness keeps us from becoming proud of our achievements, because we realize that it is only by God's grace that anything in our ministry is accomplished.

Overcomplicating Ministry Leads to a Never-Ending Search for Abilities We Don't Have

In our quest to "supersize" our ministries, we pastors often try to become something we're not. Not everyone is a hard driver and multitalented. Most of us are pretty average. We're not supersaints with superior knowledge and unusual skills and abilities. We're not great communicators who mesmerize people with our oratory skills. We're not keen thinkers who can quickly silence all doubters and distracters by giving theologically and biblically sound answers to every question. We're not superevangelists who can turn with ease any and every conversation to the gospel. We do not possess a photographic memory that can recall any verse in the Bible, and give as well an in-depth historical, cultural, and exegetical explanation of its meaning. We are not skilled musicians who can lead the congregation in resounding choruses. We are not intellectual readers who can devour and remember books by the dozen. We are not charismatic leaders who easily excite people with grand visions. For the most part, we are plain folks with average skills. What makes us unique from the rest of the congregation is not our ability but our calling. Moses was a great leader not because he had great abilities, but because he was empowered by God to accomplish God's purpose.

Despite our average skills and abilities—or perhaps because of them—we constantly feel the pressure to be like the multitalented individuals who often are held up as "the ideal pastor." Although we can appreciate the work of pastors who possess uncommon abilities, most of us are not visionaries who have the ability to conceive of and implement grand strategies and plans—nor do we need to be. But when we mistakenly shoulder the responsibility for the success of the church, we inevitably try to become what we were never intended to be. When we fall for the lie that we have to become superleaders, we set ourselves up for failure by trying to do what God has not intended for us to do. Instead of rejoicing in the tasks that God has given us, we become discouraged and frustrated.

Most of us are not five-talent individuals (Matt. 25:14–30); we're one- or two-talent people. But in the parable, the master does not condemn the servant for being a "one-talent person"; he condemns him for not utilizing the talent that he had. When we think that we have to be supertalented for God to use us, we rob him of the glory he receives when he uses us in spite of our frailties (1 Cor. 2:1–5).

Overcomplicating Ministry Leads to "Functionalization" of Ministry

The present emphasis on success has shifted the focus from leaders who *are* to leaders who *do.* Pastors are no longer evaluated primarily on character and spiritual maturity, but by what they have accomplished in terms of organizational success. Some would even say that any pastor who is not a gifted visionary—who can not build successful programs and set new directions for the church—should not become a senior pastor. Such a limiting perspective is not only damaging to the church but also unbiblical in its approach. Nowhere in Scripture is the pastoral role defined as setting the vision and direction of the church. Instead, the pastoral role is defined by the character of the individual and the importance of proclaiming the Word of God. "My interest is piqued," writes Eugene Peterson, "by living in an age in which the work of much of the church's leadership is neither pastoral nor theological. The pastoral dimensions of the church's leadership are badly eroded by technologizing and managerial influences. The theological dimension of the church's leadership has been marginalized by therapeutic and marketing preoccupations."[2] The result is that many pastors have forsaken the biblical heart of the pastoral role.

The center of the pastoral role is neither organizational (i.e., focused on vision and program development) nor therapeutic (i.e., meeting felt needs). It is theological and spiritual. Pastors are called to provide spiritual food and care for people—not to make people feel good about themselves and the world, but transform them into disciples of Jesus Christ. This objective focuses on character rather than performance; on being rather than doing. As Peterson rightly points out, "The biblical fact is that there are no successful churches. There are, instead, communities of sinners, gathered before God week after week in towns and villages all over the world. The Holy Spirit gathers them and does his work in them. In these communities of sinners, one of the sinners is called pastor and given a designated responsibility in the community. The pastor's responsibility is to keep the community attentive to God. It is this responsibility that is being abandoned."[3]

The church does not need more visionary leadership; it needs more individuals who love people and desire nothing more than to instill godly character in those people. The church needs pastors who are first and foremost biblically sound, and who faithfully communicate God's timeless truth to the culture in which we live. The church needs pastors who are more concerned about being righteous than successful. What makes pastors of small churches successful is not their ability to cast the vision for the church, but their ability to love the people in their congregation and influence them for the cause of Christ.

We must recognize, then, that God's definition of success differs radically from our own. Consider, for example, God's assessment of Omri in 1 Kings 16:21–26. Even though from a secular standpoint he was one of the most successful kings of the northern kingdom, in God's eyes he was more wicked than all who were before him. Mankind looks at results; God looks at hearts and motives. Mankind looks at performance; God looks at character. Mankind looks at accomplishments; God looks at faithfulness.

The Simplicity of Ministry

If as pastors we focus our attention primarily on strategic planning, organizational vision casting, and program development, we lose sight of the very essence of biblical leadership, which defies management and organization. Because the church is a living, spiritual organism that functions as the manifest body of Christ, biblical leadership is not complicated; it is simply the work of Christ through the ministry of the Holy Spirit.

Effectiveness in leadership does not ultimately depend on the qualities and talents of the pastoral leader, because the pastoral leader is not the most important element in a successful church. Christ is. All believers know this, of course, but do we pastors act according to our understanding? Eugene Peterson rightly points out that in order to be effective as leaders, we must first see ourselves as unnecessary. This doesn't mean that we're irrelevant, but we must recognize that there is "no *necessitas* in God."[4] God does not need us to build his church; he chooses to use us. And his primary use for us is not as organizational leaders *per se,* but as spiritual shepherds of his flock. Spiritual leadership is transformational, and the two most important elements in transforming people are the power of the Word of God (Heb. 4:12) and the power of a living model, which is primarily revealed in the living person of Jesus Christ (1 Peter 2:21). As shepherds to the flock, we as pastors are also to set ourselves as examples (1 Tim. 4:12; 1 Cor. 4:16; 11:1).

To understand the simplicity of successful ministry, then, we need to grasp the mystery of spiritual leadership. For all the knowledge gained through studies, polls, and organizational analysis, there remains a mystery in ministry that defies explanation and beggars understanding. "Unnecessary pastors need not figure everything out," Eugene Peterson writes, "but live in the awe of the God of mystery, glad to know that there is more going on than they see or can get their minds around."[5]

The writer of Ecclesiastes continually reminds us that no matter how much wisdom we as people might gain, there remains a mystery beyond the human mind's ability to perceive and understand life. We humans thus live in a paradox, at once striving to gain wisdom and become wise, yet at the same time recognizing that much of life defies wisdom (see Eccl. 9:11). So in the final analysis, we don't know what will succeed and what won't (11:6). This mystery is not the arbitrariness of chance, as some would have it, but the mystery of God (3:11).

The same principles apply to the church. Even with extraordinary insight into church and organizational leadership, there remains a mystery, an incomprehensible element that cannot be rationalized or explained, that cannot be packaged into a neat program or method that guarantees success. We humans typically do not like mysteries, because we like to exercise control and we cannot fully control that which we don't fully understand. And just as we cannot fully understand God, we also cannot fully understand his work, nor can we control what he desires to accomplish. Therein remains the great mystery of ministry.

To Understand Spiritual Leadership, We Must Recognize the Mystery of God's Work

Christ gives us a hint of the mysterious working of God when he says, "The wind blows wherever it pleases. You hear its sound, but you cannot tell where it comes from or where it is going. So it is with everyone born of the Spirit" (John 3:8). God's work is ultimately incomprehensible to humanity (see also Rom. 11:33–36). Scripture continually warns against trying to decipher the vastness of God and his work. It is not so much that we as ministers need to understand and accomplish God's purpose, will, or vision for the church; what we need to understand is that God will accomplish his purpose for the church and in the mysteries of his grace he may use us in the process.

It may be valuable at times to determine the direction of the church, but the danger of "vision casting" is that we as church leaders can become anthropocentric in our approaches, focusing on what *we* do rather than on what God is doing. Our participation is not necessary for God to accomplish his plan any more than our resistance can thwart his purposes (Job 42:2; Isa. 46:11; Acts 17:25). Thus, the most important requirement for participating in God's purpose for the church is not a clear vision but a submissive will. When we become willing vessels for God to use in whatever capacity he chooses, when we obey his Word and submit to him, God accomplishes his work through us whether we understand or comprehend his purpose or not. Likewise, Christ is not a cosmic cheerleader, rooting us on and hoping we will "win" in building the church. No, he is sovereignly active, taking personal responsibility for the health of the church. In the process, he may use us, remove us, or work around us, but he will build his church (Matt. 16:18; Eph. 5:11–16).

We give ourselves far too much credit for the success and growth of the church. The church is ultimately the work of God's sovereignty, not our best efforts and strategies. Sometimes, God accomplishes his purposes by revealing his will in very dramatic and comprehendible ways. At other times, he accomplishes his purpose when we are confused and unclear about what he is doing. Often in the pages of Scripture are found individuals accomplishing God's purposes without a clue. Instead of understanding God's "vision," they stumbled through, confused and in the dark. Paul did not understand why God prevented him from going to Bithynia. Job failed to grasp why God was allowing him to suffer. The disciples didn't fully grasp the truth about Christ until after his resurrection. Joseph of Arimathea, seeking to give Jesus a burial place, did not have in mind the fulfilling of prophecy or providing a location for the Resurrection to occur. Rather, he wanted to provide dignity to the dead Messiah.

Sometimes, God accomplished his purposes even when people sought to do the opposite of what was planned. God used the apparent rift between Paul and Barnabas to expand the kingdom. Elijah had a grand vision of the people of Israel repenting after his astounding victory on Mount Carmel. When that didn't happen, he felt defeated, but God reminded him that he had accomplished his purpose. For all the research, studies, and statistics, the bottom line is no one knows why some churches grow and some do not. We cannot even adequately define success in ministry. This is the mystery of God. In our ministries, we forget that God cannot be reduced to programs, strategies, and methodologies. He often uses them, but he is not controlled by them. As pastors of small churches, we often get discouraged because our visions do not materialize and our people do not embrace them. We become discouraged when one outreach program after another fails to attract new people. We forget the mystery of God. Perhaps God's purpose is not found in the fulfillment of our visions but in the failure of them. Perhaps God's purposes are accomplished when we think we have been the least successful (Isa. 6:9–13; Ezek. 2:5–8). Perhaps God's purposes are not being accomplished *through* us but *in* us. This is the mystery of God that we often forget. God is good, but he is not to be trifled with or manipulated. He is not a God of our creation; nor is he a God that we can manage. As Creator of all things and sovereign God of the universe, he doesn't have to conform to our expectations of what he should or should not do.

To Understand Spiritual Leadership, We Must Recognize the Mystery of Spiritual Growth

Spiritual growth cannot be programmed or manipulated. Although it is our goal in leadership to assist people in attaining spiritual growth (Eph. 4:11–13), we ultimately have no control over whether they grow or not. That's because spiritual growth is not a result of leadership; it is the work of our triune God operating in a person's heart, mind, and will (1 Cor. 1:8; 3:7; Phil. 1:6). The marvel of spiritual leadership is that God uses us to accomplish what we cannot accomplish on our own. We recognize that God uses us to change people into the image of his Son, but we also acknowledge that we can do nothing in ourselves to bring about those changes. Such is the mystery. We can see when people have experienced substantial spiritual growth in their lives, we can identify people who are spiritually mature, but we cannot explain how they attained that growth. Sometimes, if we are close enough to have intimate knowledge of someone's life, we can even see how God achieves some of the growth, but for the most part, what God uses to bring about desired changes remains an enigma.

To realize the truth of this mystery, all we have to do is look at the effect of our preaching on people's lives. Sometimes, the messages we have spent the most time preparing, the ones we communicated the most effectively, the ones we thought were surefire successes, elicit only casual yawns from the congregation. At other times, a message that we hurriedly put together, stumbled through when preaching, then walked down from the pulpit thinking was a colossal flop, is the one that has the greatest impact on someone's life. Even more mysterious are the times that people attribute their spiritual growth to a truth they learned in a sermon, yet there is no apparent connection between what was said and the impact it has on their lives. They are transformed in an area of their lives that we had no intention of addressing. Such is the wonder of the work of the Holy Spirit. In all this, however, the one constant is our responsibility to first and foremost proclaim biblical truth (Heb. 4:12; 2 Tim. 3:16).

To Understand Spiritual Leadership, We Must Recognize That God Uses Sinful People to Accomplish His Purposes

Throughout the pages of Scripture, we discover repeated testimony to the mystery that God utilizes the least likely people to accomplish his eternal purposes. God used adulterers (David), murderers (Moses), deceivers (Jacob), and the like to fulfill his plan and alter the course of human history. He used pagans who rejected him completely (Balaam), and even a donkey (Balaam's) to carry his message. Perhaps the greatest testimony of God's grace is not found in our salvation as sinners but in his utilizing us as pastors in achieving his work. Why a holy God would do so remains one of the great mysteries of ministry.

Too often, we as pastors evaluate our own spirituality and that of other pastors by the results we achieve. If someone experiences outward success, we reason, it must be because that pastor is more spiritual. Conversely, if someone struggles in ministry and fails to achieve any visible results, it must be because of that pastor's lack of spirituality. The result is either spiritual pride or spiritual judgmentalism—whether we're judging others or ourselves. If we are truly honest, however, we realize that none of us is spiritually worthy of anything God does through us. Even though others may look upon us as "great people of faith," we know differently. We know how carnal we are, how much pride corrupts our ambitions, how much we struggle in prayer, how difficult we find daily obedience. The apostle Paul, in evaluating his own life, considered himself to be the worst of all sinners (1 Tim. 1:15–16) and unworthy of his calling (1 Cor. 15:9–11). There has never been a single person in ministry who is perfectly qualified and without blemish (Luke 17:10). Therein lies the mystery of grace.

As pastors of small churches, we struggle at times with the imperfections of the people we serve. We think, *If only we had leaders in the church who were more spiritual (and more of them), then we would have a growing and dynamic ministry.* The problems resulting from these imperfections become especially acute when people on the board or in positions of leadership are not only spiritually immature but may have never experienced the redemptive work of Christ in their lives. As with the early church in Acts, we find ourselves with a congregation and leaders who have little understanding of what it means to live as a Christian and think biblically about the church. As we see in the Gospels, however, and in the book of Acts, God's grace works in the lives of people despite their imperfections and immaturity.

To Understand Spiritual Leadership, We Must Recognize That God Uses Untalented People

In our culture of success and celebrity, we ministers often have the misconception that we need to be multitalented and skilled to be successful in ministry. The tragedy of the church today is that the focus is often on talented, rather than faithful, leaders. It is assumed that the church can grow only with exceptionally gifted leaders who have certain personality traits and leadership qualities. An examination of Scripture, however, reveals a different scenario. In the early church, what often caught people's attention was the apostles' *lack* of talent and skill. When Peter and John, for example, stood before the Sanhedrin to defend their faith, the religious leaders marveled that these uneducated and untrained men demonstrated such courage and power (Acts 4:13). The apostle Paul was not a dynamic orator. In fact, people were often unimpressed with his speaking ability (1 Cor. 2:1–5; 2 Cor. 10:1, 10). But in response to the Corinthians' criticism of his personal ministry, Paul warns them against looking only at surface issues (2 Cor. 10:7). Instead of seeing his lack of oratory skills as a hindrance to his ministry, Paul considered it a key to his success, because it compelled people to base their faith on the power of God, not on Paul's talent and charisma (1 Cor. 2:5). This is not to say that God won't utilize our talents and that we should not strive to improve our skills. He does and we should. Nevertheless, we should recognize that it is not our talents but the power of God that makes us effective. The very fact that we are not supersaints, superleaders, or supercommunicators makes our ministry even more powerful, because in the end people recognize that it was God working through us that made the difference. The power of God may not completely alleviate the natural insecurities we feel in ministry, but it will make us more effective in ministry.

The church of today is not carried on the shoulders of religious celebrities and superstars, but on the commitment of countless men and women who live and serve in the trenches of daily life, faithfully communicating God's Word to the next generation. Christians owe the spread of our faith to those ordinary people who took God's redemptive message to the frontiers, who planted small, thriving churches in the far reaches of the world. Their names may never be found in the pages of a church history book, but without their ministries, the church would never have had a history to write about. Even those whose names are found in the pages of church history, those whose ministries significantly changed the course of the church, are often not the superstars we regard them to be. More likely they were common individuals placed in uncommon situations, empowered by the Holy Spirit to perform uncommon tasks. We may be unskilled in ministry, but we are never shortchanged in serving Christ. We may be like the young boy who had only a small lunch to offer Christ, yet Christ fed the multitudes with this little offering. We may not have a vast banquet table of talent to offer Christ, but he needs only that we be willing and available to give him what we have.

To Understand Spiritual Leadership, We Must Recognize the Mystery of the Church

Perhaps the greatest mystery of all is the mystery of the church itself. For all its structure, the church is not an organization. For all its strategies, it is not a business. For all its gatherings and interactions, it is not a club. And although it may be incorporated, it is not a corporation. The church is distinct from every other human institution, because at its core it is a living organism. Just as human life defies scientific explanation, so, too, the living church defies organizational explanation. The church is more than an institution—it is a living community where people live and interact with one another, and where the spiritual health of one affects the rest. Each congregation has its own history, background, strengths, and weaknesses. Each congregation has its own distinct personality, even when existing side-by-side with other churches with the same doctrine in the same community. Each congregation is also part of a greater living body, encompassing different ethnic groups, theological particularities, and cultures.

This mystery of the church's organic interconnectedness encompasses not only how one church relates to other churches, and how individuals within a congregation relate to one another, but also how the church at large relates to Christ. To be a part of the body of Christ is to be in vital relationship with the living Savior, who stands as the head of the church—this headship speaking not only of Christ's authority over the church, but also to his intrinsic relationship with the church. This union is necessary for the church to be a living organism (John 15:1–7) because Christ is the source of all life. Apart from this union, the church becomes merely a social institution, man-made and governed. In union with Christ, the church comes alive, a spiritual organization divinely established and determined.

This is true regardless of the size of the congregation, even down to the smallest church possible, where two or three are gathered (Matt. 18:20).Thus, it is not the size of the church that determines its vitality and legitimacy; it is the church's connection to the life of Christ. A church of twenty-five is as much a living expression of the body of Christ as a church of twenty-five thousand.

Every church leader must realize (and model the truth) that the life of the congregation—indeed *all* spiritual life—comes from Christ alone. This is especially true in individual churches in which the pastor isn't full-time. In this age of multiple programs and professionalism, bivocational pastors might conclude that their congregations are not "real churches" because they do not have all the ingredients—whether it be the type of music or the variety of programs—touted as essential to an effective church. But, again, the church is not about structure, or even philosophy of ministry; it is about interconnectedness with Christ and with one another.

When we as pastors lose sight of the mystery of the church and try to make ministry completely manageable, explainable, and comprehendible, we inevitably overcomplicate the church and lose sight of the essence of spiritual leadership. It is the mystery of ministry that keeps everything simple. When we grasp the vastness of ministry—and how much, therefore, we do not understand—we free ourselves to simply focus on what we are called to do: preach the Word of God and provide a living model for people to follow. We are not called to fully understand God; we are called to live in the mystery of God and marvel at who he is and what he does. We are not called to fully explain God; we are called to teach and show our people how to live in the mystery and marvel of God. That is the essence of biblical leadership.

THREE

The Necessity and Uniqueness of Biblical Leadership

The question of godly leadership in a small church is more than just idle speculation about the philosophy of overseeing people and running an organization. It addresses the fundamental responsibilities and tasks assigned to those who accept the call to pastor a small congregation. Those who enter the ministry face constant pressure to lead the church in the fulfillment of the Great Commandment and the Great Commission. To do so, we as pastors must be deeply grounded in biblical truth. We must be immersed in the Scriptures in our own lives, filtering every action, attitude, decision, and plan through the grid of God's character as revealed in the written Word. Once immersed in the Scriptures ourselves, we must carefully and clearly articulate that knowledge to the church. This communication goes beyond formal instruction on Sunday mornings. It must pervade every aspect of ministry, as pastors continually challenge people to filter all *their* actions, attitudes, decisions, and plans through the pages of Scripture. Pastors must also help other ministry leaders understand their roles, and that of their ministries, in relationship to the redemptive plan of God as revealed in the Bible.

The task of leadership involves more, of course, than just the communication of biblical truth. The responsibilities of leadership affect every aspect of the pastoral role. Small churches need more than just a good Bible scholar in the pulpit. They also need someone who can work alongside their leaders and members, expanding the ministry and influence of the church within the community. They need someone who can guide them as they walk through the minefields of change and growth. They need someone who can rally people together to work toward common goals and objectives. They need a shepherd who can bring renewal and healing when the congregation meanders into the wastelands of spiritual and organizational apathy. They need someone who can bring conflicting parties together, not only to resolve their differences but also helping them learn to love and respect one another. Small churches need leaders who can provide loving pastoral care in times of crisis. For pastors, this is the highest calling. It is an exhausting and demanding task, but one that brings joy and refreshment. It is painful yet rewarding, discouraging yet exciting. At times, it seems beyond our abilities—which is as it should be, to keep us dependent on the wisdom and power of God—but nonetheless remains necessary and worthwhile.

Defining Biblical Leadership

Even when pastors understand the spiritual basis of church leadership, it's easy to be drawn away toward the priorities of organizational leadership. We want to prod the church to achieve corporate goals, usually expressed in terms of numerical growth, program development, and fiscal plans. But as has been seen, the focus of pastoral leadership is not on management and structures and programs that minister to the masses but on relational development and personal interaction that strengthens individuals and the body as a whole. Can pastors of small churches truly be strong leaders without developing new and exciting programs? To answer this question it is necessary to be clear about the biblical concept of leadership.

Biblical leaders provide the church with a godly model to follow, and proclaim the message of God's Word in a relevant and life-changing way, so that the people of the church, individually and corporately, grow in discipleship as they influence other people for Christ. The focus of leadership in the Bible is on the spiritual transformation realized in people's lives (1 Cor. 2:1–5; Eph. 4:12). Paul, in writing to Timothy about pastoral leadership, places the emphasis on biblical proclamation and spiritual transformation: "Preach the Word; be prepared in season and out of season; correct, rebuke and encourage—with great patience and careful instruction" (2 Tim. 4:2). Notice the primacy here of the pastor's preparation. In order to transform other people, we must first ourselves be transformed. Note also the emphasis on character development, which is the natural by-product of correction, reproof, and encouragement. These are not organizational goals; they're transformational goals. And these transformational goals dictate the structure and function of the church and its leadership.

In order to be transformational, pastoral leadership must also be intentional and contextual. It is intentional in that pastors are to actively lead their congregations—preparing and preaching and prodding. It is contextual in that these primary actions are to be patiently and carefully scaled to the needs of each congregation. Because the goal is to change people, individually and congregationally, pastors must carefully think through what needs to be changed and why. They must guide their congregations in determining how to effectively implement those changes so that everyone grows in his or her relationship with Christ. To be intentional, therefore, pastors must understand the context of their churches. Contextualized leadership understands people and leads them according to where they are spiritually and organizationally (1 Cor. 9:19–23). Pastors must be students of their congregations, understanding their culture, their expectations, and their perspectives of God and the ministry. Biblical leadership doesn't force a particular model on people, but instead learns to guide people according to their characteristics and needs.

The Necessity of Biblical Leadership

Christ is, of course, the final and ultimate leader of the church, but he has assigned the care of individual congregations to pastors, who are to be "shepherds of God's flock." Without godly pastoral leadership, the church will flounder in spiritual compromise and confusion.

Biblical Leadership Is Necessary Because of the Dangers of Spiritual Compromise

In Ezekiel 34, God pronounces judgment on the leaders of Israel because of their failure to properly care for and protect the people of God. Because the shepherds (leaders) had abdicated their responsibility, the sheep (people) were scattered (v. 5). When God's people do not have godly leadership, they become easy prey for false teachers who lead them into spiritual compromise (v. 8). Every congregation needs a leader who will care for them by faithfully proclaiming God's message. Churches need pastors who understand and communicate God's Word, who point the people to Christ and assist them in attaining the fullness of Christ. The church resides in hostile territory where the enemy's sole intent is to render the church powerless. A church with no spiritual power will eventually pull away from Christ.

Scripture warns of two areas in particular where the battle for the church is being fought. The first is in the area of doctrinal integrity. Paul warns pastors of the importance of protecting and guarding doctrine in their churches and in their own lives (1 Tim. 4:16; 2 Tim. 1:14; 2:11–14; Titus 1:9). Without sound doctrine, the church is quickly set adrift in a sea of ambiguity about what it believes. In our pluralistic age, the church is in danger of becoming theologically illiterate. If that happens, both doctrinal and practical error will become rampant in the church.

The second battlefront is in the area of conduct and lifestyle. Here again, Scripture warns of two insidious errors. The first is legalism: the desire to attain God's favor through external conduct (Gal. 4–5). Our natural bent is to externalize our faith so that it becomes a cultural practice rather than an inward transformation. We are more concerned about the clothes we wear in church, the style of music we sing, or the version of Bible we use, than we are about the inward transformation of righteousness.

The second error is antinomianism, which involves the rejection of any moral code of conduct (Rom. 6). When antinomianism takes root, we find no difference between moral practices inside and outside the church. Spiritual leadership is all about helping the church steer clear of these spiritually fatal errors. Churches have a tendency to move either towards legalism or towards antinomianism. With small churches, especially those which are in isolated rural areas, the more behavior tends to be governed by legalistic and cultural norms and expectations rather than inward righteousness. As the old adage goes, "We don't drink or smoke or chew, or go with girls that do." So long as people avoid these things—or whatever other things that are proscribed—and go to church on Sunday, they consider themselves righteous.

Biblical Leadership Is Necessary Because of the Need for Biblical Teaching

Without biblical instruction, people lose the moral restraints that serve to govern their lives. One often misquoted verse on leadership, Proverbs 29:18, is taken to refer to the importance of corporate and individual vision and direction: "Where there is no vision, the people are unrestrained, but happy is he who keeps the law" (NASB). A closer examination, though, reveals that the emphasis is actually on the necessity of divine revelation and biblical truth. The term *vision* (which is parallel with *law* in the second line) refers to divine communication and prophecy and is used by Nahum as the title of his book (Nah. 1:1). Without the moral instruction of God's Word, the people abandon themselves into sin, much as Israel did at Mount Sinai (Exod. 32:25). Consequently, in the New Testament, whenever Paul addresses leaders, he emphasizes the importance of providing clear biblical instruction to the people as a foundational responsibility (Acts 20:32; 1 Tim. 3:2; 4:13; 2 Tim. 4:2). In further addressing the need for leadership, Paul sets his focus on biblical instruction rather than organizational function (Eph. 4:11–12).

The need for clear biblical instruction is even more acute today—this age in which people are inundated with information, much of which is of dubious quality. The rise of mass media and the Internet has not led to a clarification of truth, as one might have hoped; instead, it has resulted in a further dilution of knowledge as misinformation is disseminated more widely and quickly than ever. It is by no means safe to assume that just because something is found on the Internet or is mentioned in the mass media it is true. Amid this flood of information, biblical truth is often eroded by demythologization, contextualization, and redefinition by revisionists who reinterpret the Scriptures according to the norms of popular culture. To counter this trend, the church needs strong leaders who not only teach biblical truth, but who also can engage and respond to modern trends regarding biblical interpretation.

The need for leaders who can accurately teach the Bible is heightened by the general decline in religious and moral values in our secular society. Not only do people no longer adhere to Christian values and beliefs, they are ignorant of those values. Misconceptions about biblical morality and ethical standards are so widespread that, when people enter the church, we cannot assume they have even a rudimentary understanding of the fundamental beliefs of Christianity.

Biblical Leadership Is Necessary Because of the Need for Guidance Within the Church

Without a doubt, the information age has brought fresh ideas to the church. An unfortunate result is that the church—inundated with diverse ideas, programs, and strategies—often finds itself at odds with itself. Without careful thought and guidance, the church can become fragmented organizationally, and divided as different people pursue different goals. The task of leadership is to keep the congregation working together to achieve common goals. Without such guidance, small churches can easily be spread too thin as they try to accomplish a multiplicity of tasks, and they can become driven by the latest ministry fad rather than by biblical goals and standards. An examination of the effective leaders in the Old Testament—men such as Moses, David, and Nehemiah; women such as Deborah and Esther—reveals that they had a clear understanding of God's direction and possessed an ability to keep other people working toward common ends. Pastors, though, are not to dictate the direction of the church; we are facilitators, helping the church understand God's will and then keeping the people on track to accomplish those objectives.

The church, to be effective, must be unified in purpose and relationships. Effective pastors are those who can enlist the congregation's involvement and get people working together. Biblical ministry is, then, a team effort, requiring pastors to be team builders and to work as team members with their boards and congregations. Thus the task of leadership is to keep people moving in the same direction (Eph. 4:1–6; Phil. 4:2–3), not simply to achieve a corporate or organizational "mission," but in order to respond to the biblical mandate of proclaiming God's message and living out our faith in unity, in our daily lives (Phil. 3:12–14).

Biblical Leadership Is Needed Because of Constant Change in Our Society

As God moves the church toward the prophetic culmination of history, the spiritual landscape is changing at an ever-increasing rate. This constant flux in society and culture necessitates continual change within the church. Leonard Sweet warns, "The seismic events that have happened in the aftermath of the postmodern earthquake have generated tidal waves that have created a whole new world out there. In your lifetime and mine, a tidal wave has hit. We are now in transition and in transit out of *terra firma* (if ever there were such a thing) and into *terra incognita.* A sea of change of transitions and transformations is birthing a whole new world and a whole new set of ways of making our ways in the world. We have moved from the solid ground of *terra firma* to the tossing seas of *terra aqua.*"[1] Although the *message* of the church cannot and will not change, we must continually adapt the process by which we communicate the message. The church of today is not the church of the past, nor will it be the church of the future. The task of church leadership is to prepare and guide their congregations through these changes.

Rural areas in particular face significant changes. The demographic decline in the Midwest has, for example, resulted in the graying of many rural areas, resulting in an increased strain on programs and resources to help the elderly. The pressure is compounded by the flight of young people out of rural areas. The church is often the only recourse available to elderly people whose families have migrated to distant urban areas and therefore are not available to provide immediate care.

On the other end of the spectrum of change is the population growth in areas that offer natural amenities, such as mild climate conditions, topographic variation, and waterfront property. This influx has brought new challenges to the church as new ideas and expectations clash with older established patterns of church life. Along with this tension is the ethnic tension as many areas, especially in the South, have seen an influx of Hispanics seeking agricultural jobs. The result is the increase of racial tensions that rivals the inner city.

In small churches, change is often seen as an enemy rather than a friend. Consequently, pastors must carefully guide their congregations through the minefield of division and dissension as they seek to lead the people toward Christlikeness and spiritual transformation. Leaders must carefully evaluate change, in order to determine which changes are necessary and why. Wise leaders understand that all changes are not necessarily good and that some are to be rejected. They recognize, too, the cost of change and the painful process it may entail.

Biblical Leadership Is Needed Because of Misconceptions About Leadership

Small churches must approach leadership differently than their larger counterparts. Large churches tend to approach leadership from a business perspective, necessitated by their large organizational structures, with a primary emphasis on programs, goals, and objectives. Small churches, with their emphasis on relationships, are better served by approaching leadership from a family perspective, with the focus on relationships and family unity. Just as large corporations function differently from small, family-operated companies, so small churches must function differently from their larger counterparts. Many small church pastors, however, have taken the unfortunate recourse of simply adapting their leadership styles from those of larger churches. To lead a small church effectively, however, the pastor must see not only organizational connections, but also relational connections. When a pastor or leader tries to override these relational bonds, people will react negatively and forcefully. Small churches are crying out for leaders who will build fellowship even as the congregation moves toward program development and other goals.

Biblical Leadership Is Needed Because of the Necessity for Revitalization

As human beings, we become discouraged when faced with ongoing struggles and difficulties. Small churches are no exception. Often, because of the continual struggle to pay the pastor, staff programs, and evangelize the community, small congregations can become spiritually disheartened as they fail to see growth. No matter how strong a church is, it must be continually revitalized to maintain its sense of calling. It needs a leader who can not only raise the morale of the congregation but also bring spiritual revitalization. In many small churches, the people are discouraged and wondering if the church can maintain its existence. They need leaders who bring encouragement, who can guide the church in renewal, who bring a renewed and refreshed sense of God's calling and purpose. These discouraged and disheartened churches need leaders who bring a revitalized vision of who God is—and of what he can and will do through the people. Without renewal, small congregations will eventually wither as they pursue the patterns and plans of larger churches rather than simply following the Great Commission.

Biblical Leadership Is Needed Because of a Rural Crisis in America

Many of us may have a picturesque view of rural life. We visualize people living off the land and enjoying close community and a slow-paced, stress-free life. The reality, however, is often far different. Many rural areas are facing challenges and difficulties that rival the inner cities in their severity and complexity. Poverty, once thought to be primarily an inner city problem, is now rampant in rural areas. One out of four rural Hispanics, African-Americans, and Native Americans live in poverty. In 2002, one out of five children living in rural areas was classified as living in poverty. The poverty crisis is compounded by a farm crisis, which affects many rural areas, where families are losing their farms because of downturns in agronomic trends. These changes not only affect the economic well-being of families, they also create significant emotional turmoil. As Shannon Jung and Mary Agria, in a study of rural congregations, discovered, "The trauma of this economic upheaval is measured not only in dollars and cents, or bankruptcies and foreclosures. The loss of the farm is far more personal than that. It represents an emotional as well as physical hopelessness every bit as devastating as that experienced by the urban poor. The resulting stress and loss of self-esteem and identity tear at the fabric of rural family life."[2] The emotional toll has led to a significant increase of depression, alcohol abuse, and a host of other social problems that undermine families.

In the midst of this crisis, rural churches need strong, steady spiritual leadership. People in the midst of turmoil and change need to see the sovereignty of God and the reality of his work in their lives. They thus need someone who speaks biblically and prophetically to the problems they face. According to Jung and Agria, the church has been pitifully ineffective in addressing these issues. "In many communities, the church may be the single public institution still intact and able to deal with the relentless pressure on the rural family and community. Unfortunately, the church may not be assuming that leadership role."[3] Rural churches need leaders who provide spiritual perspective, who can answer questions from a biblical perspective. Otherwise, these churches will lose sight of God and his faithfulness.

Biblical Leadership Is Needed Because of a Leadership Crisis

There's no question that small churches face a crisis of leadership. Too often, freshly minted pastors view small churches as steppingstones to bigger and better things. They approach ministry as a profession to pursue rather than as a calling to develop. They treat the church as a business to expand rather than a living organism to nurture. Although they may enjoy a season of ministry in a particular congregation, they often leave to pursue a more dynamic and growing ministry. They preach faithfulness in marriage and ministry, but model adultery in their commitment to the congregation—too often leaving to pursue a more alluring and attractive suitor. After examining the shortage of pastors available to small churches, Patricia Chang concluded, "There is not a clergy shortage overall; rather, there is a shortage of pastors willing and able to serve small congregations. That is, the number of small congregations that cannot afford a full-time or fully-ordained pastor is increasing and the number of ordained pastors willing to serve in small congregations is decreasing."[4]

To be effective, pastors must first develop a biblical theology of leadership, by which they view ministry not through the eyes of one pursuing a career but through the eyes of God, who has called them to be undershepherds in the church. In God's eyes, size is not an indicator of importance or value. Every person and every congregation has equal value before Christ. Small churches need, then, the same quality of leadership as larger parishes. Pastoral leadership is not just preaching on Sundays or even developing a program throughout the week. It involves maintaining a vital connection with God so that God is accomplishing his purpose and intent through the leader and the church. As has been mentioned, leadership is first and foremost spiritual care. It means introducing people to a vital relationship with God so that people are radiant and faithful disciples of Christ. It means confronting sinners, nurturing the weak, and challenging mature Christians to new heights of growth.

This is not to suggest that we as pastors should never leave a particular church. There are times when God does call us elsewhere. But the question we too often gloss over is, why am I leaving? Is it to pursue my own professional goals, or to follow God's calling and direction?

That the church is in crisis today cannot be denied. We in the church daily face the crises of change, theological pluralism, and moral compromise. Thus, the church needs pastors who are genuine spiritual leaders, and who are not merely managers of the church's organizational functions. The church needs individuals who can do more than operate programs with efficiency and expertise;

it needs pastors who influence people and call people to be transformed into the image and character of Christ.

The Uniqueness of Biblical Leadership

To understand the type of leadership needed in this ever-changing landscape, we as pastors need to recognize that leadership in the church is fundamentally different from leadership in the secular community. If we fail to understand and appreciate these differences, we will never fulfill the desired purpose of biblical leadership. This is not to say that church leaders cannot learn much from the secular examples of leadership. We can and we should. The problem arises, however, when we equate leading the church with leading any organization. God has not called the church to be a business, or even a nonprofit organization with a social agenda. He calls us to be an organic community where people are united around common goals and a core set of values. Unlike doing business, the church is not something to be *done* (the popular phrase "doing church" notwithstanding); it is a way of life. To understand the nature of spiritual leadership, we must look beyond contemporary leadership gurus to find our instruction in the pages of Scripture. In the secular community, the leader's responsibility is to motivate and direct the group to achieve desired goals in order to deliver certain products or services. The focus is on the effect that business activities have on the *customer,* with little attention paid to the effect of those activities on the workers within the organization. Even in organizations that understand the value of "empowered" employees, the purpose and motivation of everything that organizations do is customer oriented.

In the church, the purpose is for people to live lives that will bring glory to God. God does not fill merely the role of "customer" in this transaction—he is not a "consumer" of our good works. Rather, he receives glory as the members of his church live out their faith, according to his plan, in all aspects of life. To this end, the focus in the church is *inward,* on spiritual transformation, rather than *outward,* on successful transactions, as in business. Failure to understand the distinctives of biblical leadership, or equating biblical leadership with secular leadership, leads to misguided priorities at best, or worse, the undermining of biblical leadership.

Biblical Leadership Is Unique in Its Focus

In contrast to the secular model, biblical leadership is, as stated, spiritual in focus rather than organizational. As J. Oswald Sanders rightly points out, "Spiritual ends can be achieved only by spiritual men who employ spiritual methods."[5] Spiritual leadership, then, focuses on the process rather than the product. In the sight of God, effectiveness is determined by how we pastors go about leading the church rather than by the results we achieve (Ezek. 2:5–8; 3:17–21). Paul understood the importance of the spiritual nature of leadership when he wrote that different individuals have different responsibilities, but the results are only attained by the sovereign work of God (1 Cor. 3:1–8). The focus of leadership, then, is not on human responsibility, but on God's dynamic work within the body of Christ. That work is not what we are doing for God, but what God is doing in and through us. Thus, the emphasis and focus is on God's work as he brings to full fruition his redemptive purpose. The question of leadership is not, therefore, what is most effective and accomplishes the greatest results, but what is God's will and purpose for the church.

Thus, we as pastors must recognize that the church is a spiritual body requiring spiritual means and supernatural empowerment. And because the church is a spiritual organism, how it does what it does will ultimately defy explanation. In its complexity and interconnectedness, the church is like the human body. Doctors, despite all their wisdom and skill, still encounter mysteries in the human body that they can't explain. Sometimes people die for no apparent reason; at other times, people live when every medical indication would suggest their inevitable and imminent death. In the same way that science can help us understand, to some degree, the human body, organizational methodologies can help us understand the church. But just as science cannot fully understand the nature of life and the soul of humanity, so organizational science cannot fully understand or explain the life and soul of the church.

Biblical leadership recognizes that as pastors we must look beyond the physical, visible manifestation of the church to fully understand the nature of the body of Christ. We can, in fact, only understand the church when we see it in relationship to its living connection with the person of Christ (John 15:1–17). Thus our focus must shift from the physical, visible church—as seen in its organization—to the spiritual, supernatural nature of the church—as seen in the spiritual transformation of its members.

Biblical Leadership Is Unique in Its Source

Unlike secular leaders, who are chosen by man to develop and lead organizations established by man, biblical leaders are chosen by God to oversee communities established and governed by God. Concerning the various leadership positions ordained within the early church, Paul makes it clear that each role and each person was determined and chosen by God: "It was he who gave some to be apostles, some to be prophets, some to be evangelists, and some to be pastors and teachers" (Eph. 4:11). God also determined who would be called to serve in leadership positions—such as elders and deacons—not related to specific spiritual gifts (Acts 20:28). Although the body was involved in identifying its leaders, God's unseen hand was recognized as guiding the process. When God chooses leaders, his focus is on spiritual giftedness and maturity rather than personality and talent. Just because someone is a natural leader in the business community does not necessarily mean that person is a gifted spiritual leader, even if spiritually mature. By the same token, just because someone is not a natural leader in the community or in business, and does not have the inherent personality skills of a successful business leader, does not mean that person is not qualified for spiritual leadership in the church.

Contrary to the current popular notion today, qualified spiritual leaders do not necessarily exhibit the qualities and personality traits of those who make great leaders in the secular community. The research of Roy Oswald and Otto Kroeger has convincingly demonstrated that there is no specific, dominant personality type in church leadership. Instead, the diverse range of personalities in pastoral leadership corresponds to a diversity of needs in the church, with its differing strengths and weaknesses.[6] The mistake often made is to evaluate the personality and skills of certain megachurch pastors and assume that these should be normative for every pastor. For example, these pastors, by and large, are strong visionaries; thus, the assumption is that all pastors should be visionaries. This unfortunate assumption or expectation discourages many pastors, especially in small churches, where corporate vision is an anomaly. Such expectations narrow the understanding of leadership to personality traits and talent rather than God's leadership and direction. In the end, these assumptions are a distraction from the truth—the skills and abilities that enable a pastor to be effective in a small church are vastly different from those necessary to be effective in a large congregation.

Biblical Leadership Is Unique in Its Foundation

Biblical leadership is built on a foundation of character and conduct, rather than on performance and accomplishment. Although much has already been written about character as the basis for effective church leadership, its importance can never be overstated. Most leaders who fail in ministry do so not because of misguided vision or mistakes in organizational administration, but because of moral blunders that undermine their ministries. As Joseph Stowell points out, "Ministry . . . is people working with people to produce people whose lives are solidified and unified in their Christlikeness. This is a . . . risky, unpredictable, and challenging endeavor."[7] Thus, biblical leadership demands that we as pastors lead from the context of our character. If we build our ministries on our ability to develop programs and administer organizational structures, we might have a smooth-running church but not one that transforms people into the character and mind of Christ. Who we are is far more important to the success of a ministry than what we have or what we can achieve.

"Christian leadership is unique in that it requires Christian character," writes William Lawrence. "Other kinds of leadership speak ideally of the leader's character but none of them require Christian character."[8] Further, "Leadership requires authenticity and authority. Authenticity of commitment to Christ's lordship, recognizing Him as 'Number One,' enables the leader to carry out one of his many tasks, that of being a model of Christlike maturity for those whom he leads. This authenticity makes the leader a living statement of all God wants His people to be."[9] Nor are biblical leaders just moral people who follow a consistent ethos. They are individuals who are transformed into the image of Christ and are committed to living in obedience to God's commands and precepts.

Biblical Leadership Is Unique in Its Position

Every book on leadership—including the Bible—discusses how to recognize and exercise authority. What makes biblical leadership unique is *how* it exercises that authority. The Bible makes it clear that we are to submit to authority (Rom. 13:1–3; Heb. 13:17), and that authority may sometimes be exercised rather forcefully—as in the case of Paul's various rebukes of the church in his epistles. The Bible also makes it clear that leadership authority is based on servanthood and submissive authority (Mark 10:42–45).

This responsibility of leaders to lead through submission and humility is often overlooked and neglected in our society. We as church leaders, though, are responsible to live in submission to Christ. Further, leadership in the church requires that we first recognize that we are under the authority of Christ. The New Testament writers use a number of different terms and images to emphasize that Christ is the ultimate leader of the church. He is portrayed as the head of the body (Col. 1:18), a good shepherd (John 10:14, 16; Heb. 13:20; 1 Peter 2:25; 5:4), and a husband, with his bride, the church (Eph. 5:22–33). When Jesus restored Peter to a position of leadership in the church (John 21:15–19), he did not tell the disciple to "care for your flock" or "lead your flock"; he told him to "feed my sheep." Thus, Christ makes it clear that the church belongs to him. Peter, and every other church leader down through the ages, is merely an undershepherd assigned the role of caring for Christ's sheep.

As leaders of the church, then, we are responsible to live in submission to the church. Regardless of a congregation's polity—

whether congregational or elder rule—we as members of the body of Christ are all to submit to one another. No individual stands above the rest. Paul makes it clear that the body of Christ is built on mutual equality under the headship of Christ, regardless of position (1 Cor. 12:16, 25, 27). Thus, we are to "submit to one another out of reverence for Christ" (Eph. 5:21). Further, Paul reminds the church in Rome that "each member belongs to all the others" (Rom. 12:5), so instead of elevating ourselves, we are to "honor one another above [our]selves" (Rom. 12:10).

As leaders, we must recognize that we are not experts in every aspect of ministry. Eugene Habecker points out, "It is rare that one is a leader in all dimensions of life or a follower in all dimensions of life. The reality is usually that, during any given week, one serves, alternately, and in a variety of roles, as both leader and follower."[10] Even the apostles, the recognized leaders of the early church, were accountable to the church body.

As leaders, we are accountable to the church for how we lead and where we lead. The congregation is not to blindly follow us, and neither are we to categorically demand their allegiance. Our authority to lead comes not from our position in the organizational structure of the church, but from the integrity of our lives and our message. The church should only follow us if we are following Christ, and they should adhere to our message only when we ourselves adhere to and proclaim the message of Scripture. We are thus accountable to the church for leading them into relationship with Christ.

Living in submission to the church also involves an awareness that we are accountable to the church for what we teach. When Paul preached to the Bereans, he was greatly pleased because they did not unequivocally accept his message. Instead, they evaluated his message based upon the teaching of Scripture (Acts 17:11). Rather than feeling threatened by their evaluation of his ministry, Paul saw it as a mark of maturity. We should encourage people to continually examine Scripture to see if what we are teaching is in line with biblical truth.

Finally, we are accountable to the church for how we conduct our lives. Pastors of small churches often balk at the idea of living in the proverbial fish bowl. Nevertheless, the people in our congregations have every right to examine our lives carefully. "While it's easy to resent the visibility factor of shepherding," writes Joseph Stowell, "it is important for us to remember that it is our visibility that gives us viability in the work. Were God to grant us our wish to be invisible, we might be happier, but there would be no ministry."[11] Accountability and submission do not mean, though, that we operate as leaders through popular opinion and congregational polls. At times we will need to make unpopular decisions as we strive to be faithful to our calling and obedient to God's Word. Nevertheless, we are answerable to the rest of the body and they have the right to evaluate our ministries and leadership. When pastors find themselves in difficulties, it is most often because they have failed to *listen* to people in the congregation.

Biblical Leadership Is Unique in Its Goal

In the business community, the goal of leadership is to assure the success and prosperity of the organization. In the church, the goal of leadership is the spiritual growth and success of the people in the congregation, so as to have a positive influence on people outside the church. Paul writes that leaders are given to the church "to prepare God's people for works of service, so that the body of Christ may be built up until we all reach unity in the faith and in the knowledge of the Son of God and become mature, attaining to the whole measure of the fullness of Christ" (Eph. 4:12–13). This mandate introduces a twofold emphasis in the goal of leadership: enabling others to be successful in service, and strengthening others in spiritual growth.

The goal of church leadership is not to look out for what is best for the organized church; it is to minister to each individual within the congregation. Spiritual leaders must maintain the precarious balance between the needs of the congregation as a whole and the needs of individuals. The overall health of a congregation depends, in fact, on the spiritual health and well-being of each individual in the congregation.

In the business community, output is the goal, and the bottom line is the final arbiter of success. That is, the goal determines the numbers by which the attainment of the goal will be measured. In the church, if we adopt this same output/bottom line approach, the goal quickly becomes numerical rather than spiritual. We start to measure the effectiveness of the church by the number of baptisms, the growth of membership, or the size of the budget. If the goal of church leadership, however, is to enable individuals to succeed in ministry and grow in Christ, then the "bottom line" cannot be stated in quantitative terms. The goal cannot be focused on output and production; it must be focused on promoting spiritual growth.

In business, the product is the goal and people are the means to achieve the goal. In the church, spiritually vibrant and healthy people are the goal and the "product"—that is, what the church produces in terms of programs and structures—is the means by which we change and transform people.

Biblical Leadership Is Unique in Its Empowerment

Regardless of whether leaders pastor a church or manage a business, and regardless of the size of the church or business, the task of leadership often leads to encounters with issues for which leaders are unprepared. Every leadership position comes with some level of stress, discomfort, and sense of inadequacy. When faced with difficult issues, leaders often tap into an inner reservoir to find the strength and wisdom to effectively lead the people and/or organi-

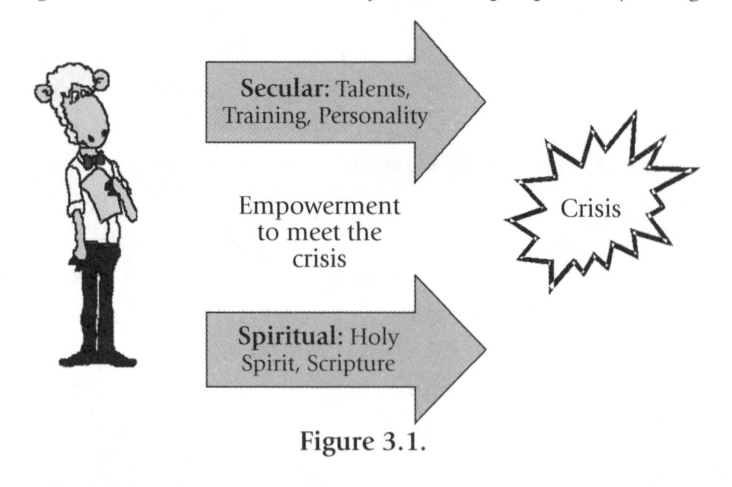

Figure 3.1.

zation entrusted to their care. What distinguishes biblical leadership from secular leadership are not the issues faced but the characteristics of the inner reservoir (fig. 3.1).

Secular leaders rely on a number of elements to empower and equip them to respond to crises. First, they rely on their talents and abilities. How capable they are often determines how far up the corporate ladder they will go. Their ability to communicate with others, remain cool under fire, and think clearly when confronted with seemingly insurmountable problems determines whether they will rise to the top or remain muddled in the middle.

Secular leaders also rely on their education and training. Warren Bennis and Burt Nanus write, "The truth is that major capacities and competencies of leadership can be learned. . . . Furthermore, whatever natural endowments we bring to the role of leadership, they can be enhanced; nurture is far more important than nature in determining who becomes a successful leader."[12] The "reservoir" of education includes formal education, specific training, lessons learned through experience, and the counsel of others who have faced similar problems.

Secular leaders rely on their personality traits. Effective leaders are often those who have a type-A personality, are driven to succeed, and possess a clear vision. They are highly disciplined individuals who know how to accomplish their tasks and achieve their goals. Because of their strongly motivated nature, they can overcome many obstacles simply by working harder and being tenacious in their pursuits.

The inner reservoir of successful spiritual leaders may or may not include some of the same strengths that work for business leaders. Although some leaders in the pages of Scripture manifest strong corporate leadership skills, many do not. In the early days of the church, the religious leaders were, in fact, so unimpressed by the qualifications of the disciples that they marveled at the impact they were having in Jerusalem (Acts 4:13). In the eyes of the Sanhedrin, the disciples were nothing more than common folk, uneducated and ordinary. Yet they established a living body of believers that is still vibrant today. Why the success of the church? Gamaliel, one of the

Jewish religious leaders, announced prophetically—although not intentionally so—that if the church was empowered by man, it would ultimately fail; but if it was empowered by God, nothing could stop it (Acts 5:35–39). Even Paul, who had all the natural and educational advantages of his day, recognized that the success of his ministry was due to spiritual empowerment rather than personal skills or innate abilities: "My message and my preaching were not with wise and persuasive words, but with a demonstration of the Spirit's power, so that your faith might not rest on men's wisdom, but on God's power" (1 Cor. 2:4–5).

Those words are especially comforting for those of us who serve in small congregations and feel inadequate to lead. We do not have the multiple talents, gifts, and skills of some of our brethren in larger churches, nor are we gifted communicators. Even if we were to attain positions as senior pastors of large churches, we would quickly flounder under the weight of the task. We can, however, lead with confidence the churches that God has entrusted to us, not because we are talented or educated, but because we have the Holy Spirit's empowerment. We have the assurance that we are always sufficiently empowered to accomplish exactly what God has called us to accomplish. Success in pastoral leadership is not determined by education—although it is valuable and important—or personality or talents, but by the Holy Spirit working in and through us.

Along with power of the Holy Spirit, biblical leadership is empowered by its message. Programs, as important as they are, do not bring about transformation. The leader's skills, abilities, and personality do not change people. What changes people is the power of the message of Scripture, which penetrates the soul and brings about both redemption and sanctification (Heb. 4:12).

Biblical Leadership Is Unique in Its Priority

In secular business, families are often sacrificed on the altar of success. To rise to the top, leaders must work many hours and spend less time at home. They must remain focused on business issues and not be distracted by outside concerns. It is tragic that many church leaders have adopted this same philosophy. George Barna reports,

"One out of 10 [pastors] admits that [his] family has suffered greatly as a result of current church ministry; another 4 out of 10 note that their church work has made life at least somewhat more difficult for their family."[13]

Ministry is demanding. No matter how hard a pastor works and how many hours that pastor spends in ministry, many needs are left unmet. Pastors live constantly with the guilt that somehow they have not done enough. When parishioners leave for another congregation, we as pastors feel guilty for neglecting them. If the church is not growing, we feel guilty that we have not spent more time with the unsaved. No matter how much we do in the church, there is always more that could be done. We could always lead one more Bible study, spend one more night out in visitation, develop one more program. All these ministry opportunities, coupled with the pressure to succeed, can lead us to sacrifice our families. If our wives complain that we have not spent any time at home with them, we piously answer that we are busy doing "the Lord's work." We may even think that, because we are devoting ourselves to ministry, God will take care of the needs of our wives and children. Apparently, it never occurs to us that God might want us to care for our own families.

The apostle Paul set a different priority for those who aspire to be leaders in the church. He said that leaders in the church must first be leaders at home, and failure to do so would disqualify one from ministry (1 Tim. 3:4–5). The idea that someone would sacrifice his family for the sake of ministry was not only foreign to Paul's thinking, it was contradictory. If we pastors have become so busy in ministry that we no longer have time to meet our families' spiritual and emotional needs, we need to rethink our priorities. Robert Anderson warns, "Next to his relationship with God, there are no more important relationships than those of a husband and wife and a father and his children. Those relationships must be preserved and enhanced at all cost."[14] Within the secular community, the success of leaders is not predicated on their relationships in the home. In the church, no pastor can succeed if he has failed to be the spiritual leader at home. This is not to say that pastors must have perfect children who are dynamic and outspoken in their faith and never have any spiritual doubts and struggles. But pastors who desire to be biblical leaders will strive to maintain a healthy balance between the demands of ministry and the demands at home. A pastor's "relationship to his family [must be] as high and as sacred as that to his church."[15]

Biblical Leadership Is Unique in Its Approach

The call to leadership in the church is a call to a life of service. In contrast to the secular community, in which employees serve the leaders and the corporation, within the church the leader serves the people. Our task as leaders is not to get the people to accomplish our goals, but to support the people in accomplishing their goals as God has equipped them. Our task is "to prepare God's people for works of service" (Eph. 4:12). In writing this, Paul places the emphasis on servant ministry. Thus, a leader's presence in the church is a supportive ministry. This pattern is not a new standard of ministry; it merely follows the example established by Christ. One of the profound mysteries in the Bible is that Christ, the creator of the universe, became a servant of humanity (Phil. 2:7). This mystery has enormous implications for those who aspire to leadership. What Paul ordains for everyone is especially true regarding biblical leaders: "Do nothing out of selfish ambition or vain conceit, but in humility consider others better than yourselves. Each of you should look not only to your own interests, but also to the interests of others" (Phil. 2:3–4).

Pastors who have not learned the importance of being servants to the congregation find themselves in trouble. If they come into a church with an idea or an agenda—often based on what will make them successful—that the church does not embrace, they may become cynical and critical. They may condemn the church for being spiritually lazy or stubborn. They may criticize the church board for being unspiritual or satisfied with mediocrity. But typically the one thing they have not done is listen to the people and their desires and dreams for the church. The vast majority of people in a small church want to see the church grow and see people come to Christ;

what they disagree on is the process by which it should be done. When a leader becomes a servant to help others achieve their dreams, the people will rally around the pastor and support that pastor's ministry.

Biblical Leadership Is Unique in Its Motivation

Motivation is the driving force behind action. It defines why we humans work, why we devote ourselves to a particular task, and the sacrifices we are willing to make to achieve our goals. Students of human behavior and business management have identified several motivational factors that affect a person's commitment and willingness to sacrifice for a specific goal. They include recognition, competency, achievement, personal growth, and challenge.[16] Other factors include financial security, power and authority, career advancement, or personal goals. A person's motivations ultimately relate to his or her personal goals and well-being.

These basic motivational factors are not necessarily evil or undesirable; church leaders, however, are called to be motivated by a higher incentive: to glorify God. What Paul says about all believers is, again, especially true for church leaders: "Whatever you do, work at it with all your heart, as working for the Lord, not for men, since you know that you will receive an inheritance from the Lord as a reward. It is the Lord Christ you are serving" (Col. 3:23–24). Everything we do is to be done in the context of our relationship with God. Biblical motivation is not psychologically, economically, or personally driven; it is theologically and spiritually driven. We are not performing tasks for personal gain but working for the advancement of God's purpose and plan. In ministry, it is easy to be motivated to serve for financial gain, personal recognition, or career advancement. Many small churches have, tragically, suffered because of these unbiblical motivations. Many pastors view small churches not as valid places of ministry but as necessary stepping-stones for the development of their careers. They regard small churches as places to start in ministry in order to gain enough experience to move on to larger churches, or places to retire in order to maintain an income without the pressures and programs of a larger church.

Our motivation as pastors is often further revealed in our response to difficulties and conflicts in the church. Some pastors are quick to judge—and leave—a church if they feel the people are not responding as they should to the demands of Scripture. When confronted with unhealthy churches, many pastors are quick to leave and shake the dust off their feet, rather than patiently working to bring those churches back to spiritual health. We often forget that we are not called to pastor healthy churches filled with perfect people. Every church is unhealthy in some way, and every church is filled with spiritually sinful people—of whom we are one. Our calling is to serve the people and equip them "for every good work," by proclaiming the Word of God, and thereby "teaching, rebuking, correcting and training in righteousness" (2 Tim. 3:16–17).

As pastors, we are not to be motivated by our own agendas and desires, but by what pleases God and glorifies him (Ps. 115). Faithfulness, rather than success or security, should govern our activities. We are not to be concerned primarily with our personal plans and purposes, only with proclaiming Christ to a dying world, regardless of our churches' size and setting. We must realize that success and security in ministry have nothing to do with us and everything to do with Christ.

> What, after all, is Apollos? And what is Paul? Only servants, through whom you came to believe—as the Lord has assigned to each his task. I planted the seed, Apollos watered it, but God made it grow. So neither he who plants nor he who waters is anything, but only God, who makes things grow. The man who plants and the man who waters have one purpose, and each will be rewarded according to his own labor. (1 Cor. 3:5–8)

As pastors, examining our motives is often the most painful and difficult aspect of ministry, because we realize that our primary motivation is not the desire to exalt Christ but the desire to attain our own personal goals and desires. Because our society values pleasure, ease, and safety, we make decisions and take actions that alleviate hardship and minimize risks. But God has not called us to lives of ease and safety, either physically or economically; he has called us to live by faith through self-sacrifice, faithfully serving him regardless of the hardships and struggles we encounter.

In the business world, motives are overshadowed by achievements. As long as leaders produce the desired bottom-line results, no one cares about what motivates them. But in the church, why we do what we do is far more important than what we achieve. We may do "all the right things" and achieve visible, measurable results, but if our motives are skewed, then in the end we have accomplished nothing (Matt. 6:1–8). From God's perspective, our motives matter as much as our actions.

Biblical Leadership Is Unique in Its Devotion

Loyalty is virtually nonexistent in the secular world—and it is a two-way street. Employees are no longer loyal to a particular company because the company is not loyal to them. Companies hire, fire, and relocate employees in order to achieve corporate goals, without much consideration of the effect those changes have on employees. Likewise, most employees will change jobs if better opportunities come along, regardless of the effect their leaving has on their former companies. It is increasingly rare for employees to work for one company throughout their careers—and companies don't expect them to.

Although a lack of loyalty is accepted as normal in the workplace, it is not acceptable in ministry. As pastors, we often decry the lack of commitment in our congregations. We condemn the consumer mentality that plagues the church, in which people change churches as readily as they change the oil in their cars. At the first sign of trouble or dissatisfaction, people jump ship to go to a church that "better ministers to my needs." As pastor Erwin Lutzer rightly points out, "Like the nominally religious, we choose what we will believe and how we will act without much concern for what the Bible teaches. Carl F. Henry wrote, 'Millions of Protestants, many evangelicals among them, choose and change their churches as they do their airlines—for convenience of travel, comfort, and economy.'

For us, as well as for the world, it's religion a la carte."[17] As pastors, we often do, however, the very thing we condemn. We're no more loyal to a particular congregation than the people are themselves. As soon as a better offer comes along, we're ready to jump. "During the past two decades," reports pollster George Barna, "the average tenure of senior pastors has dropped to about four years from seven."[18] Furthermore, the "data indicate that the smaller the church body the more likely the pastor is to spend only a few years in that pulpit."[19] These findings are especially distressing in light of all the evidence that the most productive years of a pastor's ministry come after three years. Gerald Gillaspie warns, "All who are concerned—pastors, churches, and denominational leaders—should aim to do everything in their power to allay the prevailing spirit of unrest and to alter the practice of the continual, frequent, and unwise sundering of pastoral relations."[20]

The call to leadership in the church is a call to be devoted and faithful, just as the God we serve is inherently faithful in all he does. To reflect the image of Christ in our ministries, we pastors must reflect his faithfulness to us. God does not abandon us as his children when we do not follow his leadership. When mankind rebelled, God did not simply make another world in order to have a better "congregation." Instead, he lovingly remained, standing by his people even though they had forsaken him. Rather than destroy humanity, he carefully and patiently sought to guide and protect us as we discovered the beauty of his design and the joy of his salvation. As church leaders, we are called to demonstrate this same faithfulness and devotion to God's people. This is not a blind devotion that ignores problems and overlooks faults; rather it is a principled devotion that provides loving care and steadfast guidance as we patiently work with people in the church to develop greater godliness.

Biblical Devotion Involves a Love for the Universal Church

Ephesians 5:25–33 is often referred to in the context of marriage; Paul's primary focus in this passage, however, is not the marriage relationship but the attitude that Christ has for the church (v. 32). To be a servant of Christ involves a deep love and commitment to the universal bride of Christ. As pastoral leaders, we are to serve the church because we are passionate about presenting to Christ a bride that is radiant, "without stain or wrinkle or any other blemish, but holy and blameless" (v. 27). We serve, not because of financial remuneration or personal reward, but because we desire to do nothing else (1 Peter 5:2–4) Our loyalty is not to denominations—as valuable as they are—or to theological systems—as important as they are—but to the person of Christ and the advancement of his kingdom. Without this loyalty, we will be more concerned about building "our church" than his church. If we are not concerned about the universal church, we will see other congregations as rivals rather than as coworkers in a common cause.

Biblical Devotion Involves a Love for the Local Church

Our love for the church is foundational for the growth and well-being of the church. It is not enough to love some of the people in the congregation, or even all the people in the congregation. Rather, we need to be passionately in love with the church—the people, the programs, the facilities, the culture. In explaining this kind of love, David Hansen draws a distinction between church leaders and secular leaders when he writes, "Sure, it's better if teachers, doctors, and artists love the people they work with. But they can perform their work without love and they can even do it well. The bind we face is that we can't do pastoral ministry without love. It isn't a series of tasks we do *with* love—rather, pastoral ministry is love, which we apply with a series of tasks. Preaching, teaching, calling, praying, even church administration are nothing but the consistent application of God's love to the church."[21] Without this kind of love, a pastor will never bond with the congregation, never become a part of the church body. "When a church and a pastor do not bond," David Hansen continues, "the church cannot grow—in numbers, in commitment to one another and to God, to mission, to worship, and to a deeper spirituality. The simple reason is that all growth involves change and risk, which causes most individuals and all congregations profound anxiety and threatens to keep us from taking the steps to growth."[22] The difference between pastors who love the church and those who don't is the difference between a true shepherd and a hireling (John 10:1–18). Loving the church means we will sacrifice ourselves for the church, protect the church from destructive forces, and respond with grace and compassion to the faults and weaknesses of its people. When we genuinely love the church, we will not become embittered by our experience in the church. We will avoid the cynicism that often strikes pastors when churches don't grow spiritually or numerically at the desired or expected rate. We will not divorce our congregations because larger congregations offer us jobs with bigger salaries.

Biblical Devotion Involves a Love for Each Individual Within the Church

It is usually easy to love most of the people in a congregation, because most people appreciate the work we pastors perform and respond to our ministries and leadership. It is always the case, however, that certain individuals are difficult if not impossible to get along with. Every small church—and large church, for that matter—will have some people who are dissatisfied with the pastor's ministry. Most will remain quietly in the background and never raise a ruckus. A few, however, will be vocal and subversive, letting the pastor and everyone else know that the ministry of the church is not measuring up to their expectations.

In every congregation, too, certain individuals require constant pastoral care as they continually struggle with emotional, spiritual, and psychological problems. Even after countless hours of counseling, they still require ongoing attention and involvement. They frequently call, regardless of time of day, to unload their burdens as they face each new crisis in their lives. They demand a large amount of their pastors' time and spiritual and emotional energies. In a small church, such individuals have direct access to the pastor, who often doesn't have the luxury of assigning them to another staff member or lay leader.

Nonetheless, we are called to love and remain committed to even difficult and challenging people. Loving the church involves loving every individual in the church, regardless of how we are treated in return. Our love for the church is measured not by how we treat the people who treat us well, but by how we treat those who treat us poorly. Do we provide them with the same spiritual care? Are we as willing to spend time with them as we are with anyone else? Even as Christ was dying on the cross at the hands of jealous religious leaders, his love for them was evident when he prayed that the Father would forgive them for their act of hatred. As his undershepherds, we are to model Christ's love, even for our enemies. Only then will our message have true power and authority.

Biblical Leadership Is Unique in Its Task

Unlike the business world, where the focus is on building organizations, pastors are called to build communities where people can reach spiritual maturity. In business, interpersonal relationships are important only insofar as they help a company achieve its goals. A business can function productively and remain healthy even if the people are motivated by personal gain—for example, salary, promotions, benefits. But a church cannot thrive when its members focus solely on self, and are led by selfish motives. That church will self-destruct. In the church, the task of leadership is to transform people from their natural independence and self-centeredness to self-sacrificing interdependence. People may enter the church with selfish motives and not much concern for others, but within the church they must learn to set aside their own selfish agendas in order to serve others (Phil. 2). The task of leadership is to challenge people to practice self-sacrifice and promote mutual edification.

FOUR

The Foundation of Leadership

Most pastors arrive at their first parishes with a mixture of excitement and apprehension. They believe that their schooling has supplied many of the foundational tools needed to develop a healthy church—and it has—even though there is still much to learn. They recognize that pastoral ministry is more than a job or a career; it is a lifelong pursuit that began when they first sensed God calling them into ministry.

It doesn't take long for most pastors to realize there is much they are still not equipped to deal with. They may have arrived at their churches, thinking that all they need to do is provide exegetically sound sermons relevant to the needs of the people, but it soon becomes evident that the role of pastor involves much more. They realize that to be effective pastors they must also be effective leaders. Consequently, they begin to read as much as they can about leadership and management. But these books and articles, instead of providing the answers that pastors seek, often leave them feeling even more defeated and discouraged as they struggle to live up to the standards for success presented by the authors. They also soon discover that most small churches are not interested in goals, objectives, and action plans. They are not expecting their pastors to develop new programs and implement lofty visions; instead, they want their pastors to spend time with them and work with them in dealing with issues in their lives. They don't want organizational leaders; they want relational pastors who guide them in their spiritual pilgrimages.

The result for many pastors is confusion concerning their roles and functions. To alleviate this confusion, pastors must go back and reassess the foundation on which biblical leadership is built. When they reexamine what Scripture says, they discover that the basis and foundation of biblical leadership is not established on their educational qualifications, their management skills, or even their position in the church as outlined in the church constitution. Notice in figure 4.1 that the foundation for biblical leadership lies in the call of God, and in the leader's godly character and spiritual reliance on God.

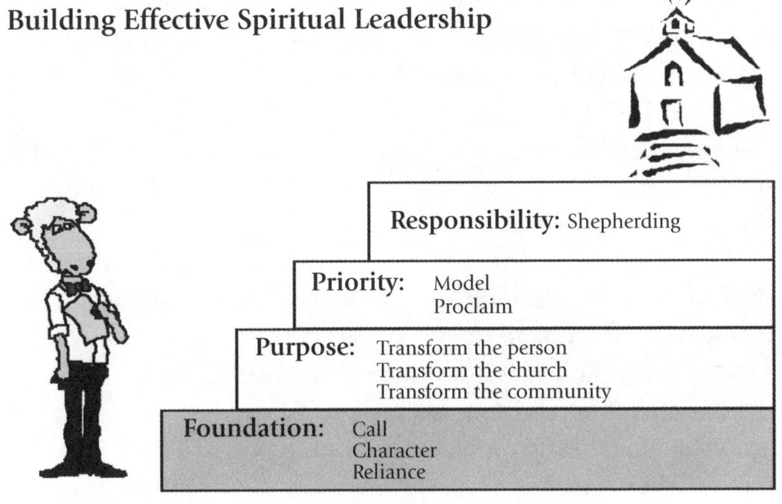

Figure 4.1.

The Foundation of Leadership Requires the Call of God

The idea that one is called into ministry has lost popularity in the modern church. Often we ministers view the ministry as a career we've chosen to pursue rather than as an irrevocable and unrelenting calling by God. Scripture tells us, however, that God is the one who initiates our pursuit of ministry.

God Establishes the Position

The roles and responsibilities of pastoral leadership are not organizational necessities invented by the church. The position was established by God for the purpose of guiding and protecting his people. Leaders in the church are people who are appointed by God to serve the church by assisting others in attaining God's purposes for their lives and ministries. This task is not defined by a church constitution or a job description developed by a church board; it is defined in Ephesians 4:11–16, where Paul describes God's purpose for appointing various individuals to lead the church. A similar leadership structure is ordained for the marriage relationship, in which God established husbands as heads of the home. Headship in the home, though, does not mean that the husband controls the home; rather, he is to serve his wife and strive to lead her toward spiritual maturity (Eph. 5:22–33). The biblical concept of leadership, both at home and in the church, dictates that leaders are called to serve the needs of others. The focus is not on who makes the decisions and determines the direction for the church—or the family—but who serves the congregation—or the family—in order to equip and strengthen the members in their spiritual lives and ministries.

Within the pages of the New Testament, God-ordained leadership is neither organizational nor authoritarian, although it certainly involves authority; God-ordained leadership is based on sacrificial service. In the biblical model, the pastor serves the people by helping them achieve their spiritual goals of Christlikeness and Christ-centered ministries. In doing so, the pastor's position is not so much *over* the church as it is *under* the authority of Christ. The pastor is not the head of the church. The church has only one head, and that is Christ (Col. 1:18; Eph. 1:22). Thus the pastor is a servant under the authority of Christ, and given charge over the care and spiritual growth of the body. The authority of leadership derives, then, from the authority of Christ, not organizational position. Too, pastors have authority to the degree that they fulfill God's purpose for ministry. If they stray from God's purpose and plan, they no longer have authority in the church. Because God did not call pastors to lead the church but to serve the church under Christ, Christ determines the roles and responsibilities of leadership. He has revealed these roles and responsibilities in Scripture. Consequently, as pastors we must look to Scripture to discover our purpose.

God Appoints Pastors to Fill the Position

The foundation of a pastor's call to ministry is the general calling of all Christians to a life of service (Eph. 2:10).[1] Thus the focus of ministry is not so much on the process as on the purpose (1 Cor. 12:18; Rom. 12:1–2). Scripture tells us that when individuals were chosen by God for ministry, they were chosen for a distinct purpose in ministry (e.g., Paul in Acts 9:3–6). As the one who calls us into ministry, God has specifically assigned and equipped us with spiritual gifts to be utilized within the church. Thus, a leader is more than a person who holds a particular position within the church; a leader is spiritually gifted by the Holy Spirit for the purpose of leading the congregation.

The role of pastor is based, too, on more than a particular skill or personality. In studying the leaders that God uses in Scripture, it is seen that no particular personality trait stands out. Some leaders were dynamic and charismatic; others were plain and uninspiring. Some were doers; others were thinkers. Some were forceful; others were quiet and unassuming. The only common trait is that each leader had an unabashed passion for God's reputation and an unwavering desire to obey him. As William Lawrence rightly points out,

> The gift of leadership is not a matter of a certain personality type. Peter was a leader by virtue of personal strength (Acts 4:8–12), James by virtue of practical wisdom (Acts 15:12–21), Paul by virtue of intellectual capacity (as seen in his sermons and epistles), Timothy by virtue of sacrificial service (Phil. 2:19–21), and John by virtue of his heart for God and man (as seen in his writings). All these leaders shared all these virtues, but each of them had a distinct personality strength that uniquely marked him. This demonstrates the fact that leadership is not a matter of human personality but of divine sovereignty. Just as the Spirit's gifts are not reserved for a few outstanding people, so the Spirit's gift of leadership is not reserved for a particular kind of personality.[2]

It can be overwhelmingly disheartening and discouraging when pastors enter the ministry, comparing themselves with other pastors, some of whom exhibit specific personality traits and possess multiple gifts and talents. Those of us who serve in small churches often wonder if we're even cut out for ministry because we're not drivers by nature but are more relational. Yet, according to Scripture, God uses all different types of personalities to lead his people—sometimes within the same leadership team. Paul, for example, manifested a driven personality, whereas his traveling companion Barnabas was highly relational. The very qualities that make some pastors effective leaders in small churches would hinder their effectiveness in larger churches. As pastors of small churches, we need to relax in ministry, realizing that God has not only called us to serve him in our small churches, but he has also given us the right gifts and personalities to effectively lead our congregations toward maturity.

In seeking to understand our call to ministry, then, we must recognize that our calling is based on God's sovereign choice rather than on the decision of a particular congregation. We are not leaders because we are popular, or because we are talented, or because we have attended Bible colleges or seminaries; rather, we are leaders in the church because of God's sovereign work in our lives and in the church (1 Cor. 12; Eph. 4:11). Thus, our calling is not subjective; it is based on an objective reality. And because God is the one who calls, our vocation is divinely initiated, not based on human wisdom. We are pastors not simply because we regard the job as a viable career option and because we enjoy helping people. We are pastors because God, of his own initiative, has called us.

Further, the pastoral vocation is a lifelong calling. In Romans 11:29, Paul places our call to service parallel with God's elective call, and he describes them as being irrevocable.[3] Although our ministries may change and the avenues by which we express our gifts may change, our calling to service remains a lifelong commitment. Too often, pastors approach ministry as if it were merely an occupation, engaged in for a period of time, then left behind for a new means of employment. God has called us to a higher task. He has called us to remain faithful to him and to our service. Thus we must, as must all believers, present ourselves as living sacrifices, offering God complete control of our daily lives (Rom. 12:1–2).

The implications of these verses are enormous for our approach to ministry. To be a living sacrifice requires complete dedication to God for his use. The idea is not so much that our sacrifice is intended to appease God, but that because we now belong solely to God we're not to be used for any profane purpose. In the Romans passage, however, Paul sets up a paradox; the term he uses for "sacrifice" is a word that refers to a burnt offering rather than a living sacrifice. The point is that we are to live our lives continually as if we were dead, that is, we are to consider ourselves dead to our own lives and living only for God and what pleases him. As a result, we are to remain persistent in the face of difficulty (Rom. 5:3–5; 2 Tim. 1:8). The call to ministry is a call to suffering, and we are not to leave the ministry solely to alleviate the suffering we will face. Instead we are to remain faithful, serving God no matter what the cost.

The church today is in desperate need of pastors who are living sacrifices. The church needs pastors who understand their calling and who are willing to go where God leads them, unconcerned about the problems they will encounter. The small churches that today face a crisis of leadership do so not because of a shortage of available leaders, but because of an acute shortage of pastors who are willing to serve in a small church. Patricia Chang, after an extensive study of the problem faced by many denominations concluded that "the real problem denominations face is not a clergy shortage generally, but a shortage of pastors who are willing and able to serve the small congregation."[4] When pastors no longer see ministry as a high calling but only as a career option, small churches, which offer little financial reward, will suffer as a consequence. When pastors no longer see ministry as a divine calling, they will be drawn instead by financial incentives, location and size of a congregation, breadth of programming, and opportunities for advancement. In many ways, we pastors have sold our birthright of ministry for a bowl of career pottage.

The church needs pastors who not only have a sense of calling, but who also are not concerned about expanding their careers or building a greater financial portfolio in order to gain greater financial security. Small churches desperately need pastors who see the value of each individual in the church, and who recognize that our calling as pastors is to serve the body of Christ, no matter how small or out of the way that part of the body may be.

God Equips the Person to Fulfill the Position

There's not a single person in ministry who at times does not feel overwhelmed by the task. This is especially true in rural areas where mental health services and government financial assistance are not readily available, and people look to the church—and to pastors—to fill the gap. Nothing in a typical seminary education prepares a pastor to handle people who are in the midst of emotional breakdowns, who can turn only to the local church for help because there are no other services available. Nothing in a typical seminary education prepares a pastor for the financial struggles that people face in rural areas, where the poverty rate exceeds that of the inner city. Nothing can prepare a pastor for the crisis of dealing with a pregnant teenager, parents grieving over the suicide of a child, or the death of a baby from SIDS. Yet these are the crises to which pastors are often called to respond. In many rural areas, the local pastor is looked to not only for biblical instruction, but also for emotional and mental counseling. As a result, rural pastors are often faced with their own inadequacies and limitations.

At times like these we as pastors of small churches feel the full weight of our inadequacies. But at times like these we must remember what it is that makes Christian leaders unique from leaders in other enterprises: we are empowered by the Holy Spirit to fulfill our calling as pastors. When we serve with the recognition that we cannot perform all the tasks we've been assigned, we become most useful to God, because we no longer rely on ourselves but on God's strength, wisdom, and guidance. And God never calls us to a task that he will not fully equip us to perform.

The Holy Spirit takes responsibility for equipping us for ministry, utilizing a variety of means:

1. He equips us through the impartation of spiritual gifts, the means by which we accomplish the ministry of leadership in the church. We are pastors not because the church needs someone to fill the role, but because we have been gifted by God to be pastors and teachers.
2. He equips us through instruction and training, both individual and systematic. This instruction begins with preparation in the interpretation of Scripture, the most essential element of our ministry (2 Tim. 3:16–17; John 16:13). The understanding and application of Scripture becomes the basis by which we utilize the power of the Holy Spirit in leading the church. The most important training we receive in seminary is not the "practical ministry" courses, but the courses in biblical interpretation and exegesis. These are the courses that enable us to properly understand the truth and build a right theology of God.
3. He equips us through his divine presence. Christ assured his disciples—and us—that he would not leave them without assistance as they fulfilled the Great Commission. Thus, he sent the Holy Spirit to empower and enable the ministry of the church (John 14:26–27). The Holy Spirit brings to mind the Scriptures necessary to deal with situations that we encounter in ministry, guiding us to effectively communicate the Word of God. His continual presence is the most important ingredient in our ministry as pastors.
4. He equips us through spiritual growth. Because ministry is an outgrowth of maturity, the deeper our understanding of God and obedience to him, the greater our impact will be. This growth is not a work we do within ourselves; it is a work that God does within us (2 Tim. 1:6–7; Phil. 1:6). This spiritual growth is seen not only in our development of godly character, but also in the growth and development of our spiritual gifts through use and practice. The more we utilize our spiritual

gifts, the greater our effectiveness will be as God builds ministry skills into our lives.

5. He equips us for success. In our success-oriented society, we often forget that our ultimate success in ministry does not depend on our abilities but on the faithful work of the Holy Spirit through us (1 Thess. 5:24). In small churches, we often struggle and feel cheated in ministry because we do not have all the resources at our disposal that larger churches have. We become discouraged because we feel that God has called us to a ministry without fully equipping us to accomplish it. We need to remember, however, that God has provided for every contingency. Because he is omniscient, he knows everything—every possibility and every solution. Because he is omnipotent, he possesses the power in himself to fully accomplish his purpose. Because he is omnipresent, he is always with us in the process, guiding and directing as we fulfill his plan.

Regarding this last point, when we evaluate our success in ministry, we must adhere to God's definition of success rather than to our own. In a small church it's easy to question our effectiveness in ministry because we often do not see the desired outward results. True success, however, is ultimately found in faithfulness and obedience rather than in numbers and achievements. We need to recognize that we can't fail when we obey God's revealed word, strive to be submissive to his will, and remain faithful in performing the tasks set before us (Matt. 25:21). Our effectiveness, remember, is based on the Holy Spirit's accomplishment of his purpose through us, not on our own abilities and accomplishments (1 Cor. 2:1–5).

The Foundation of Leadership Is Godly Character

Throughout the New Testament, leadership is based on godly character. In our pragmatic contemporary culture—where accomplishments define success and abilities, and talents determine qualifications—it's easy to forget that the only qualifications for leadership outlined in Scripture are spiritual giftedness and character. As pastors, we stand or fall in ministry based on our character. Regardless of our other achievements, a flawed character will disqualify us from leadership in the church. Godly character involves both right conduct and right doctrine (1 Tim. 4:16). If we live right but have wrong doctrine, we're heretics. If we have right doctrine but fail to live rightly before God, we're hypocrites. Godly living stems from God-centered theology that governs all that we are and do.

Leaders Demonstrate Godly Character in Relationship to God

Before we pastors can be qualified for leadership, we must first have and maintain a right relationship with God, which is based on a mature understanding of doctrine. Paul, in his writings to Timothy and Titus, reminds them—and us—that personal commitment to Christ and obedience to his Word are at the heart of the Christian experience. Contrary to popular culture, which has abandoned all semblance of theology, one cannot live rightly before God without correctly understanding who he is, which is the essence of theology. Thus Paul writes to Titus, "Hold firmly to the trustworthy message as it has been taught" (Titus 1:9). Doctrine has been maligned, however, as unnecessary and even divisive within the church. The pitiful result is that pastors often view theology and doctrine as something to be discussed by theologians in the halls of a seminary, but impractical in daily life and ministry. Without a biblical theology as a basis for life and ministry, however, the church is reduced to a social organization that operates programs rather than being a vital, living body that challenges people's hearts and minds with biblical truth; pastors become CEOs, who oversee programs, rather than proclaimers of truth.

Second, to have a right relationship with God we must be able to communicate and model Christ to others. An essential component of spiritual maturity is the ability to communicate God's truth to people. When Paul states that we are to be "able to teach" (1 Tim. 3:2), he has more in mind than just publicly communicating the Word of God. Rather, he is referring to the ability to instruct others in spiritual truth—either formally or informally—and refute false teachers (Titus 1:9). The ability to teach combines the understanding of truth with the ability to demonstrate to others the relevancy of Scripture to life. Teaching may include preaching and other public proclamation, but it also includes informal and private interactions.

Third, leaders must have spiritual integrity, which is consistency between what we believe about God and how we live (Titus 1:8). This consistency springs forth as an expression of character, not because of congregational expectations and pressures to conform to external standards, but as transformed by the person of Jesus Christ. In a small church, the pastor's life is an open book. People can easily recognize when pastors are play-acting—preaching one thing and living another. This is not to say that we must be perfect, but we cannot teach what we cannot model. If inconsistency is evident between our message and our lives, we will lose the respect of the people and the platform of our ministry.

Fourth, to have a right relationship with God, we must be faithful stewards who are approved by God (Titus 1:6–7). One of the dangers in a small church is that pastors can become relationally driven, where decisions are based on political expedience rather than on biblical principles. Even pastors can be governed by the desire to please others rather than God. There may be times when as leaders we'll have to make unpopular decisions that are necessary based on biblical instruction. Although it is important in a small church to be relationally sensitive, we must always remain biblically directed.

Fifth, we are to demonstrate maturity and growth. When Paul states that an elder is not to be a recent convert (1 Tim. 3:6), *recent* emphasizes one who has not yet matured spiritually. As leaders, we must be not only firmly grounded in truth and practice, but also consistently growing in our faith.

Finally, as God's representatives, we must be passionate for righteousness. Our ultimate desire, that which drives our decisions, must be an intense longing to see the honorable and the good become predominant, both inside and outside the church. We are not to have a micro vision of ministry, focusing only on what is happening within the church. We are also to have a macro vision of ministry, seeking to promote goodness throughout the whole community.

Leaders Demonstrate Godly Character in Relationship to Others

One of the hallmarks of a transformed life is an intense and unconditional love for others (John 13:35). This love is radically different from the attitudes demonstrated in the world. We are not just to overlook others' faults, but also to have a genuine concern for their well-being—even for those who consider themselves our enemies.

To have right relationships, we must live in such a way that we gain respect (1 Tim. 3:2, 7)—both within the church and the community. Regardless of whether others agree with us, or even like us, we should live our lives such that they cannot speak negatively about us. Our conduct should be such that people will acknowledge our character even if they reject our faith (1 Peter 2:12, 15). This is especially important in rural communities, where church leaders are highly visible. People will long remember the momentary slips that undermine our reputations in our communities. It is equally true that we will gain a hearing within the community if we demonstrate consistent godliness in our characters.

A godly character includes hospitality in relationships (1 Tim. 3:2; Titus 1:8). As our society becomes increasingly fast-paced and depersonalized, people long for meaningful interpersonal relationships. A strength of a small church is that it is a place where people can form close, personal relationships, and find mutual encouragement and accountability. These same close relationships, however, can be a small church's greatest weakness, if people fail to open up warmly to newcomers. Often this aloofness is not intentional, but when people's relational needs are already met, they do not always take the initiative to build new relationships. Thus, our task as pastors is to take the lead in "adopting" new people into the church family.

To have right relationships, pastors must also demonstrate skill in resolving conflicts. Conflict is a part of life and a part of leadership. Leadership involves constantly introducing people to the need for personal, spiritual, and organizational change. Change inevitably leads to conflict as the old clashes with the new. Wise leaders are those who respond to conflict not with further hostility, but who strive lovingly and properly to resolve the conflict (1 Tim. 3:3). This doesn't mean that we church leaders pursue peace at all costs, for we cannot compromise truth. It does mean that we are gentle in our dealings with others, and when challenged, we respond with grace, compassion, and humility rather than with hostility and aggression.

A further essential ingredient of godly character is a humble attitude toward ourselves and others. Paul warns against being "overbearing" (Titus 1:7), referring to one who is self-pleasing and self-willed. As leaders, we are not to be inflexible in our opinions, demanding our own way and using the power of our position to accomplish our personal agendas. Instead, we are willing to respect and listen to others' viewpoints and ideas; we're willing to serve, to seek the best interests of our congregations rather than our own. This means that we do not view our small churches as stepping-stones to larger congregations. Otherwise, we have become self-pleasing, elevating ourselves rather than humbly serving our congregations.

A final element of right relationships with others is our having a right relationship with money. A preoccupation with money inevitably breeds corrupt motives and fraudulent activities (1 Tim. 6:10). Many pastors, for instance, base their acceptance of a calling to a church solely on the financial package the church offers. Although we need to be wise stewards and sensitive to the needs of our families, we should never be motivated in ministry by financial remuneration. Rather, we are to serve willingly, basing our future security not on what we possess, but on God, who cares for our needs.

Leaders Demonstrate Godly Character in Relationship to Family

Stated bluntly—and it needs to be—no man should be a spiritual leader in the church who is not first a spiritual leader at home. Thus, anyone who desires to lead at church must first model godly servanthood with his family. We pastors must recognize that our families come before vocation, and the needs of our families before our own careers. Paul makes it clear, in fact, that an essential qualification for leaders in the church is that they serve as pastors first to their own families. We might fool a congregation into thinking we are spiritual; we might hide behind organizational wisdom and wear a nice suit on Sunday to appear devout, but we cannot fool our children or our wives regarding our faith. If we are not living with integrity at home, they will not follow our footsteps to the church.

This means that a pastor must be committed to his wife (1 Tim. 3:2). Although there has been much debate concerning the exact nature of the command, the focus of the verse is clear: to be effective in leadership, we pastors must be consistent in our moral integrity and faithful to our covenant relationships. This goes beyond sexual purity and includes emotional faithfulness as well. Many pastors who would never consider sexual adultery have committed emotional adultery. Their mistresses are not other persons, but jobs, careers, hobbies, or anything else that has supplanted or subordinated their loyalty and commitment to their spouses.

Godly character also involves a commitment of pastors to train our children. Ministry should never be an excuse for neglecting our relationships with our children. Paul even says, "If anyone does not know how to manage his own family, how can he take care of God's church?" (1 Tim. 3:5). As William Hendriksen points out in his commentary on 1 Timothy, "It must be done in such a manner that the father's *firmness* makes it *advisable* for a child to obey, that his *wisdom* makes it *natural* for a child to obey, and that his *love* makes it a *pleasure* for a child to obey."[5] Too often, the focus of pastoral success is on a pastor's performance and accomplishments in the church rather than at home.

Leaders Demonstrate Godly Character in Relationship to Themselves

Leaders in the church must recognize their responsibility to control their natural desires and feelings. They must be governed by the truth of Scripture rather than by cultural norms and expectations, or by their natural inclinations. Small churches often have a set of cultural norms that govern people's behavior—including the leader's. As long as a person adheres to these expectations, they are deemed acceptable. These norms may be expressed in the way people dress on Sunday, activities they choose or shun (no movies or dances), or the manner in which they conduct the worship service (hymns with a piano or organ, but no drums). As pastors, we must look beyond these cultural expectations, making decisions and controlling our conduct based on biblical truth.

As leaders, we need to check our desires toward self-centeredness, laziness, sexual temptations, gluttony, and any other habit that can hinder or distract our work for Christ (James 1:13–14; 1 Cor. 9:27). Our identities and worth are found in God, and our satisfaction and joy in life flow from our relationship with him. These outcomes occur when we are controlled by the Holy Spirit rather than by any external stimulants (Titus 1:8; 1 Tim. 3:3; Eph. 5:18). An effective leader, then, is governed only by the will and purpose of God. The danger for we small-church leaders is—even though we may not use such stimulants as alcohol—we can become controlled by tradition and popularity rather than by the Holy Spirit. Tradition plays an important role in small churches as it provides continuity and a relational connection between generations, but problems arise when tradition controls decisions and governs the ministry of the church. When this happens, the pastor must not be afraid to stand up and break with tradition. We must be more concerned about following God's leading and direction than we are about popularity.

Demonstrating godly character means that we are also careful thinkers (1 Tim. 3:2; Titus 1:8).[6] We are not rash in our judgments, jumping to conclusions about plans, ideas, or people. Instead, we carefully think through issues and seek all the available information. We should not immediately reject an idea just because "we tried that once and it didn't work," or "it has never been done that way before." Neither should we accept an idea simply because "an expert says it should work." Rather than following fads, we must carefully examine each issue, based on the foundation of Scripture and our understanding of our specific cultural setting.

Further, to be godly leaders, we must set the standard by being good stewards of our personal finances. As has been stated, the proper motivation for our service is based not on what we get out of it but on our love for God and our desire to serve others. The motivation to accumulate money solely for ourselves will cloud our perspectives so that we make decisions based on what is good for our savings accounts rather than on what is best for God's kingdom. Ministry, after all, involves sacrifice—of our time and our money. As elders, we must maintain a proper perspective of money, recognizing that it is a tool to be used for God's glory rather than something merely for our own enjoyment. That may at times need to be manifest as a willingness to sacrifice our resources for the needs and good of others.

The Foundation of Leadership Is Spiritual Reliance

When we enter the pastorate, we often view our education as the basis and foundation of our ministries. Having obtained a degree and some training, we feel fully equipped to serve effectively. When we encounter perplexing issues and problems in the church, we turn to the latest seminar or book to find the answers. Not to minimize the importance of education and ongoing training, but they can lead to a sense of self-sufficiency in ministry, based on our own qualifications and abilities. In Scripture, however, the apostles approached ministry differently. For them, the foundation of their transformational ministry was reliance on God. When Paul approached the church at Corinth, it was not with the eloquence of a highly trained rabbi, but in humility and the power of the Holy Spirit (1 Cor. 2:1–5). And prayer was central to all he did. So, too, the apostles in Jerusalem, when faced with the increasing demands of ministry and the administrative challenges confronting the early church, made sure that prayer remained the priority of their time and energies (Acts 6:4).

Today, in our methodological approach to ministry, we often neglect prayer. As Eugene Peterson points out, "In twentieth-century America, the prophetic pastor of action and the managerial pastor are the ministry role models; the prayerful pastor leading people in worship draws, at best, a yawn."[7]

Prayer Is Central to Our Ministries

Often we approach prayer the same way we approach visitation or preaching; as a task that is simply part of the job description. As a result, we view prayer as a duty to perform rather than as an attitude of reliance on God to govern all of our activities. We try to keep time for prayer on our schedules, but the other demands of ministry often get in the way. Pastors are never lacking for things to do, many of which demand immediate action and attention, and despite our best intentions, our prayer time often gets shoved to the background. Meanwhile, in seeking the key to ministry we are continually looking for the right method, program, or vision for the church.

Norman Shawchuck and Roger Heuser, in speaking of the need for congregational renewal, said, "If your church is dying, name it for what it is, and then set about with abandon to see whether you might find the Golden Thread that holds promise of immediately breathing new life into the gasping body. . . . When the congregation is dying, something must be done, and it must be qualitatively different from what has gone on before. The Golden Thread never is to be found in the bin marked 'business as usual.'"[8] For Shawchuck and Heuser, the "golden thread" is a new program or approach to ministry that brings excitement and vitality to the church. Although an argument can certainly be made that a struggling church can benefit from innovative new ideas, it should not be at the expense of the most important ingredient of any ministry. The golden thread will not be found in an innovative program or new approach to ministry; the golden thread is prayer. A reliance on prayer is a recognition that we do not, and never will, have all the answers for ministry. It is sad, indeed, that we have largely lost this focus in ministry, and thus we have compromised our complete reliance on God. John Piper challenges us when he writes, "A pastor who feels competent in himself to produce eternal fruit—which is the only kind that matters—knows neither God nor himself. A pastor who does not know the rhythm of desperation and deliverance must have his sights only on what man can achieve. But brothers, the proper goals of the life of a pastor are unquestionably beyond our reach. The changes we long for in the hearts of our people can happen only by a sovereign work of grace."[9] For this very reason, reliance on God through prayer is essential for effective ministry. In Scripture, prayer is the first and central work of every effective leader. Moses established a nation with the recognition that he was inept but God was capable, thus leading him to a life of prayer (Exod. 4:11–17; 8:30; 10:18; Num. 11:2; 21:7). Nehemiah built the walls of Jerusalem on the foundation of prayer (Neh. 1:4–11; 2:4; 4:4–5; 6:9). The apostle Paul continually made prayer central to his ministry. If prayer is not the central foundation on which we build our pastoral ministries, then we are like a truck stuck in a quagmire, making a lot of noise and throwing up a lot of mud, but going nowhere fast.

Prayer Recognizes a Life of Dependence on God

Prayer is not a form of manipulation whereby we tap into a supernatural power supply that guarantees the success of our dreams and plans. Prayer is recognition of our need for God to act. Prayer is both an action and an attitude. It is an action in that it is something we are to do, but it is also an attitude that is to govern our lives. When Paul exhorts the church to "pray continually" (1 Thess. 5:17), he is not suggesting that we as believers pray twenty-four hours a day. Rather, he is calling us to an attitude of complete dependence on God's action and the work of his grace in everything we do. Jesus himself identified the importance of total dependence when he said, "The Son can do nothing by himself; he can do only what he sees his Father doing, because whatever the Father does the Son also does" (John 5:19). Jesus did not come to do his own will but the will of the Father (John 6:38). For us as pastors to live in dependence on God involves the recognition that we need his strength, his wisdom, his empowerment, his guidance, and his direction in order for us to be effective in ministry.

Prayer Is the Avenue Through Which God Works

Perhaps the greatest mystery of God's activity is that he condescends to limit his activities through the prayers of his people. As John Piper points out, "Prayer is the coupling of primary and secondary causes. It is the splicing of our limp wire to the lightning bolt of heaven. How astonishing it is that God wills to do His work through people. It is doubly astonishing that He ordains to fulfill His plans by being asked to do so by us."[10] This is the puzzle that has confounded even the greatest theologians.[11] While affirming God's sovereignty, we also affirm his choice to limit at times his activities to what we pray for (Ezek. 36:37). He invites us to ask of him, and he assures us that he will respond. Prayer is the means by which God works in our lives. If we are to be transformed by Christ into the ministers he desires us to be, then we must pray for God's will to be done in our lives. Prayer is the means by which God gives us boldness to proclaim his Word (Col. 4:3–4). Prayer is also the foundation for our calling. We are called to ministry in response to prayer (Matt. 9:38). But prayer is foundational for God's work not only in our own lives; it is also foundational for God's work in the life of the congregation.

Prayer Is the Means by Which We Have Spiritual Influence

The apostle Paul, throughout his ministry, saw a close connection between prayer and the influence of his ministry. Whenever he wrote to the churches, he couched his letters in prayer. His effectiveness in guiding the church through the minefields of spiritual growth was directly related to prayer. As leaders, we must do more than preach and teach the word, visit the sick, and organize ministries; we must first and foremost be people of prayer. The prophet Samuel also saw the connection between spiritual leadership and prayer. He saw prayer as so foundational that the failure to pray was a direct violation of God's purpose and will for him as a leader (1 Sam. 12:23). We cannot be spiritual leaders if we are not spiritually focused, and we cannot be spiritually focused if we are not committed to regular prayer. We cannot afford to be haphazard or arbitrary; our prayers must be specific and continual. One of the greatest advantages we have in a small church is the opportunity to pray for the specific needs and issues confronting the members of the congregation. Our ability to serve their needs is vitally connected to our prayers for them. Prayer is not a duty to *perform;* it is the very lifeblood of our ministry. Like the disciples who themselves became the answer to the prayer for more workers (Matt. 9:35–10:1), we will find that our ministry to the church is a response and an outgrowth of our prayers. In the prayer closet, we gain both the wisdom and the motivation to minister to people's needs.

Prayer Is the Means by Which We Discern God's Will

Ultimately, the success and effectiveness of our ministries will not be determined by numerical growth or outward results. The final test of our ministries is our obedience to God's will. If we are aligned with his will, we are effective regardless of the apparent results. It is significant that Peter received the vision concerning the inclusion of the Gentiles in God's program during a time when he was isolated in prayer (Acts 10:9). Before Jesus chose the twelve disciples, he spent the night in prayer (Luke 6:12–16). Often we struggle to know God's will because we fail to pray for direction. When we pray, God gives us greater clarity and understanding of his will. It is a great misdirection that, all too often, our prayers are simply requests for God to bless our plans, rather than to enable us to see *his* plan. Living a life of dependence on God means we seek his face regularly and continually to understand his purposes.

Praying for the Congregation

- √ We are to pray for people's spiritual growth (Eph. 1:17).
- √ We are to pray that people will have right perspectives of life (Eph. 1:18).
- √ We are to pray for love and unity in the church (Phil. 1:9).
- √ We are to pray for the church's spiritual discernment (Phil. 1:10).
- √ We are to pray that people might be pure and blameless (Phil. 1:10).
- √ We are to pray that people will know the will of God (Col. 1:9).
- √ We are to pray that people's conduct might be pleasing to God (Col. 1:10).
- √ We are to pray that people will fulfill God's purpose (2 Thess. 1:11).
- √ We are to pray for the physical and emotional needs of people (James 5:14; 3 John 2).

Prayer Is the Means by Which We Survive the Pressures of Ministry

Ministry is pressure packed. None of us who has been in ministry for any length of time is without spiritual and emotional scars. The pressure is further compounded by our isolation. It is sad that many pastors of small churches do not have anyone with whom to confide or share struggles. Henry Blackaby and Richard Blackaby describe the predicament of many small church pastors: "Because of their position, most leaders carry a heavy load of responsibility. It may be difficult to find someone with whom they can share their concerns and fears. Sometimes, circumstances dictate the need for complete confidentiality, so the leader bears the weight of responsibility alone."[12] This sense of isolation is further compounded for pastors in remote, rural communities, because they not only have no one in the church with whom to share their fears, they also have no other pastors nearby to serve as sounding boards and give perspective to difficult situations in the church. Paul acknowledges the pressures of ministry when he writes, "When we came into Macedonia, this body of ours had no rest, but we were harassed at every turn—conflicts on the outside, fears within" (2 Cor. 7:5). Often it is those "fears within" that torment pastors the most: fear of failure, fear of a loss of income, fear of rejection, and fear of incompetence. Added to these fears is the pressure of dealing with concerns for the well-being of the church. We can empathize with Paul's statement in 2 Corinthians 11:28–29: "Besides everything else, I face daily the pressure of my concern for all the churches. Who is weak, and I do not feel weak? Who is led into sin, and I do not inwardly burn?" In light of these pressures, we pastors can easily become depressed and discouraged. Peter, however, provides the key for dealing with the stress of ministry: "Cast all your anxiety on him because he cares for you" (1 Peter 5:7). As Blackaby and Blackaby point out, "When leaders allow Christ to carry their emotional and spiritual loads, this takes enormous pressure off them and allows them to face even the most difficult assignments with peace."[13]

As pastors, our calling, character, and prayer life are central to our leadership. We can possess all the natural leadership abilities that would make us successful in business, but if we are not called to ministry, if we lack character, and if prayer is not the centerpiece of our lives, we will never be effective for God. Conversely, we may not be outstanding leaders from the world's perspective, but if God has called us, if we possess godly character, and if we're devoted to prayer, we will be effective leaders in the church. The most effective leaders are not those who dream lofty dreams, set ambitious goals, and develop efficient programs. They are not those who speak eloquently or reveal keen insight in strategic problem solving. The most effective leaders are those who possess a deep love for Christ and the church, who have a thorough understanding of Scripture and can apply the Word of God to the issues confronting the church, who have been called by God to serve him, and who are devoted to prayer in pursuit of God's will. Those who are successful in ministry recognize that the foundation of ministry is not their abilities, but is a life of dependence and daily reliance on God. Effective leaders are those who follow Christ wholeheartedly and are shaped by his character in such a way that God shapes others through them.

Figure 4.2. Foundation for Effective Ministry

FIVE

The Purpose of Leadership, Part 1

The Call to a Transformational Ministry

To understand leadership, we must understand its fundamental purpose. It's been said that if you don't know where you're going, you'll probably end up somewhere else. Likewise, if we don't have a clear idea of our purpose as church leaders, we will never be certain of what we're supposed to do. How we understand the purpose of leadership will determine how we define the task of leadership and how we perform the responsibilities of leadership. Purpose defines goals; goals define priorities; and priorities define daily responsibilities. If we see our purpose as leaders as organizational, our goals will center on developing proficient organizations, our priorities will be those things that contribute to an efficiently run organization, and we will define our responsibilities according to the needs of the organization. If, on the other hand, our purpose as leaders is spiritual—which, according to Scripture, it is—our goals, priorities, and responsibilities must be spiritually defined.

As illustrated in figure 5.1, the spiritual purpose of leadership is to bring people into a personal, vibrant, and real relationship with Jesus Christ. Paul describes the purpose of his ministry in Colossians 1:28–29: "We proclaim him, admonishing and teaching everyone with all wisdom, so that we may present everyone perfect in Christ. To this end I labor, struggling with all his energy, which so powerfully works in me." For Paul, the purpose governing all his activities and efforts was the spiritual transformation of people. And this spiritual transformation governs our purpose as well. Because the purpose of church leadership is to bring people to Christ, our goal is to lead in a manner that brings transformation to people's lives. People must be transformed—in fact, radically changed—to enter into a vital relationship with Christ. They must be changed redemptively—that is, changed from spiritual deadness to spiritual life through salvation in Christ—and they must be changed sanctificationally, an ongoing process by which they begin to manifest and reveal Christ's character. This task, though it ultimately rests on the initiative of the Holy Spirit, involves the work of spiritual leaders. Paul states emphatically that God gave leaders to the church for the purpose of assisting the church in this sanctificational process (Eph. 4:11–13).

Both the purpose and the goal, then, of spiritual leadership is transformational. Spiritual leaders are not to lead passively, merely imparting knowledge about God in the hopes that people will respond. Instead, we are to actively and assertively seek to influence people for the cause of Christ. Too often in our preaching, we have presented theology on its own merits, but without a transformational goal. Although our theology, our study of God, has been systematic and well-reasoned, it lost its power and influence because it was often presented without a corresponding call to respond properly to God. It addressed the mind but not the will. It challenged how we think about God, but neglected to challenge how we live before God. As a result, people came to the wrong perception of theology as dead orthodoxy, a tragic assumption, indeed, in light of proper theology's being a necessity for vibrant spirituality. Today, we face the same danger with regard to church leadership. When we start to view leadership as primarily organizational (i.e., vision casting, administration, programs, etc.) we lose the very soul of leadership. The leader's principle task is not to challenge people's minds with biblical facts—although this is necessary—nor is it to guide the church's organization—as important as this is. Rather, the leader's principle task is to challenge people to be transformed by the proclamation and application of biblical truth (Acts 2:40; 26:3, 28–29; 2 Cor. 10:1–2; Gal. 4:12). When we lose sight of the transformational purpose, goals, and priorities of spiritual leadership, we render our leadership impotent and stagnant. Consequently, the people in the church become cynical and apathetic toward their leaders.

The Necessity of Transformational Ministry

Crucial to our understanding of transformational leadership is the realization that all transformation is ultimately the work of the Holy Spirit in the lives of individuals. In the end, we must recognize that our own efforts in changing people are not worthy of recognition or merit. All credit, glory, and honor go to our sovereign and gracious God, who works mightily in people's lives. Equally crucial is the realization that God, in his infinite wisdom and grace, chooses to use us as leaders in the process of effecting change in the church. He calls us, equips us, empowers us, and uses us for transformational ministry. Transformational ministry is crucial because people do not come to the church spiritually whole—they come spiritually and morally marred and crippled.

We Are Called to Lead People in Spiritual Transformation

The world is in a crisis of confusion concerning the character and nature of God. Just as paganism and polytheism tainted the ancient Near Eastern world, our society is influenced by corrupted views of God. The names have changed, but the false gods they represent have not. Instead of Baal, we have New Age philosophy; instead of the sun god Ra, we have Eastern mysticism, with its worship of creation; instead of Asherah, we have the worship of supermodels and the sexuality they represent. Instead of idols made of silver, gold, and wood, we have consumerism, materialism, humanism, yoga, meditation, and a host of other philosophies that draw from the same cesspool of idolatry represented by the gods of the Canaanites.

Like Israel in the times of the prophets, our culture has incorporated modern idolatry into our view of spirituality. Our culture's renewed interest in spirituality has not, sad to say, resulted in a clarification of biblical truth for most people. Instead, truth is now seen as relative, and the common understanding of the nature and being of God has become clouded and confused. Like the prophets of Scripture, our task as spiritual leaders is to call people away from the confusion of polytheism to the clarity of the monotheistic God of Scripture. Like Elijah on Mount Carmel, we are called to challenge people to choose between the God of the Bible and the gods of the culture. We are called to confront erroneous notions of God and to rebuild a proper perspective and a right understanding of him. Transformation begins, then, not with changing people's perspective of themselves, but with changing their perspective of God.

Even though we pastors know our people well in our small churches, we should never assume that they have a right understanding of God. Many people who come to our churches Sunday after Sunday, who have been raised in our congregations, who wouldn't dream of reading any other Bible but the King James Version, have idolatrous views of God. As Stephen Charnock points out, it is not the absolute denial of God that lies at the heart of atheism; it is the denial or doubting of some of the rights of his nature.[1] Idolatry is not only the denial of the God of Scripture in favor of another; it also is the misrepresentation of him. If we as pastors are not actively seeking to correct people's view of God, in effect we deny the exclusiveness of God and the vitality of his nature—and we become idolaters ourselves.

We Are Called to Lead People in Moral Transformation

Along with a distortion in how God is viewed comes a distortion of how morality is viewed. It should not surprise us that we see a moral decline in our culture; it is the inevitable result of postmodernity. When truth becomes unknowable, morality becomes indefinable (1 Tim. 1:10–11). Morality and ethics are further undermined when our focus as a society shifts from personal character to personal achievement. As Millard Erickson points out, "The effect of this modernization is to create two separate spheres, the public and the private. The one world is defined by personal relations, and is made up of small, insulated islands of home, family, and personal friends.

The other is defined by the functions within the capitalistic machine. In this great system of production and distribution, persons are valued not for who they are or what they believe or hold as values, but for what they do."[2] The tragedy is that what is true in our culture is equally true in the church. No longer are leaders evaluated by the values they represent, but by their achievements. As long as a pastor is well liked, communicates effectively from the pulpit, and "builds" the church, people are willing to overlook significant moral and ethical weaknesses.

Along with this moral decline comes a whole new set of moral questions. Genetic engineering, artificial reproduction technology, doctor-assisted suicide, right to die, and a host of other ethical questions brought about by scientific advances have raised a new set of moral issues. Other issues that have long been present in specific subcultures are now becoming prevalent in the mainstream of society. Problems such as gambling (now supported by the state), pornography (both soft- and hardcore), civil disobedience, drug abuse (both alcohol and other substances), divorce, and a host of other social concerns are no longer outside the church. We live in a society where self-centeredness and manipulation are encouraged (consider, for example, the proliferation of "reality" TV shows on which people are willing to hurt, embarrass, and manipulate others for personal gain) and humility and community are abandoned. It should be kept in mind, then, that just because a person comes to church doesn't mean that he or she has left behind the cultural morality—or immorality—to embrace a biblical morality and ethos.

It is in this world as described above that we must provide spiritual leadership. As we lead, we must challenge people to transform their morality not by merely confronting cultural vices; we must call people to become completely different. As Carl Henry points out, "Christianity is qualitatively different or it has nothing distinctive to offer the world. . . . We need to do more than to sponsor a Christian *subculture.* We need a Christian *counterculture* that sets itself alongside the secular rivals and publishes openly the difference that belief in God and His Christ makes in the arenas of thought and action. We need Christian *countermoves* that commend a new climate, countermoves that penetrate the public realm."[3] The transformation to which we are to call people must be complete and entire, affecting the very core and essence of their personhoods. Concerning this transformation, Paul writes that believers are to become new creations (2 Cor. 5:17). This is not merely a restoration of people by the Holy Spirit to a pre-Fall condition, but a complete transformation that penetrates the very nature of the individual. The result is believers who think differently, having a completely different mind-set (Rom. 8:5–7).

Becoming a Transformational Leader

Thus, inherent in our calling as small church leaders is our mandate to transform people. Although transformation is ultimately the work of the Holy Spirit, we have the distinct privilege of being used by him to work in people's lives. It is important, therefore, that we be available to the Holy Spirit to be used. Availability involves not only our inward willingness to serve, but also our preparation and development as leaders.

A Transformational Leader Is a Student of Culture

To speak effectively to the issues and misconceptions of our society, we must understand the culture in which we live. All humans are products of our various cultures. Culture influences and governs our thinking far more than we realize. If we were raised in the United States, for example, we will think and react much differently than a person raised in an Islamic culture. Even within a distinct culture, people's morality, values, and lifestyle will be affected by divergent subcultures. An individual living in an innercity subculture will view life differently from a person raised in a rural setting. People from the South have different values than people in the Pacific Northwest.

As church leaders, we can embrace cultural values only insofar as they support biblical values. Where cultural values are neutral—such as in matters of style, dress, and music—we can and should remain neutral. But where culture violates biblical values and teachings, we must confront and challenge these values from a biblical perspective. To distinguish between these different levels of cultural involvement, we must have a thorough, Spirit-guided knowledge and understanding of our surrounding cultures. We must then be able honestly to assess our cultures from a biblical perspective. Because, though, we are always influenced by our cultures, it is impossible to be absolutely culturally neutral. Nonetheless, we must strive to step outside our cultures, reexamining our cultural expectations and values by the standards of Scripture.

1. To step outside of culture, we must be thoroughly biblical in our perspective. The difficult challenge we face is that we often read our cultures into the pages of Scripture instead of using Scripture to evaluate our cultures. Often our view of God, our view of morality, and our view of ourselves, is determined more by our cultural perspectives than by a solid biblical belief. Thus, the challenge is to allow Scripture to speak for itself. This is especially difficult in rural areas, where community and church cultures are often more homogeneous and play a far more important role in people's lives than in urban or suburban areas.
2. To step outside of culture, we must be critical of our cultures. Because we are products of our cultures and we take our cultures everywhere we go, including the church, it can be difficult to see where our cultural norms are unbiblical. For example, in rural areas, the individualism and self-reliance that characterizes many people make it difficult for them to realize the importance of community and interdependency among the people of God. Furthermore, in small churches, the stress on and importance of relationships can often override the governing principles of Scripture. So, for example, people are reluctant to conduct church discipline, even if it is mandated clearly by Scripture. As church leaders, we need to understand and be critical of our cultures in order to separate cultural values from biblical truth.
3. To step outside of culture, we must listen to the voices of outsiders. We can learn a lot about what is good and bad in our

cultures by listening to people who are not a part of our cultures. We often turn a deaf ear to people who are critical of small churches, because they do not understand the small church and rural community. Their criticism may be unjustified because they fail to understand the dynamics of the community. Their criticism can, however, also convey elements of truth that can challenge our cultural biases. Before we dismiss them as outsiders, we should listen to them.

A Transformational Leader Has a Clear Perspective of God's Design for Individuals, the Church, and the Community

To lead effectively, it is necessary to understand what God wants to accomplish in transforming people and the church. As leaders, we must continually search and examine the Scriptures to determine what God wants the church to be and how the church is to be involved in the community. To be transformational leaders, we must recognize the three groups of people we are called to influence: individuals, the church, and the community at large.

Most ministry is done one-on-one and face-to-face with individuals. We must strive, however, to preserve a balance between individual and collective ministry. We should never place the ministry needs and priorities of the community above those of individuals, just as we should never place the ministry needs of individuals above those of the community.

The tendency in a small church, because it is relationally driven, is to focus so much on individuals that it damages the well-being of the collective church. Because of relational connections with others in the church, for example, people are allowed to have positions of leadership even though they are not spiritually qualified. As leaders, we must move the collective church toward spiritual wellness in order to move individuals to spiritual maturity.

We are called to redemptively influence the community as a whole by pointing people to Christ and by being a positive moral influence in the community. Christ reminds us that we are the salt of the earth; that is, we are a moral and spiritual preservative hindering the influence of paganism and immorality in society. We are not called to live in isolation from the community, but to exist as part of the community, presenting the reality of Christ within the daily thoroughfare of life.

A Transformational Leader Is Personally Transformed

We cannot lead where we have not gone, and we cannot transform others if we ourselves are not being transformed (Jer. 5:5). The greatest challenge we face in ministry is not what we do in relationship to the church; it is allowing the Holy Spirit to do what he wants in our own lives. The disciplines of study, prayer, self-examination, and personal discipleship are essential to the pastoral role. We may be able to run an efficient organization without prayer and an intimate relationship with God, but we cannot transform other people that way. If we are not ourselves being transformed, we will inevitably fall prey to the same snare that trapped the leaders of Israel who became more concerned about their own well-being than about spiritually nurturing the people (Jer. 23:1–2, 16–18).

Building Effective Spiritual Leadership

Responsibility: Shepherding

Priority: Model
Proclaim

Purpose: Transform the person
Transform the church
Transform the community

Foundation: Call
Character
Reliance

Figure 5.1.

Transformational Leadership: Transforming People

In a small church, if we start trying to duplicate what worked somewhere else, we can quickly become focused on programs and structures and lose sight of the real object of our ministries. If we attempt to become mini-megachurches, instead of developing ministries tailored to the needs of our specific location and environment, we may fall prey to the proverbial error of the tail wagging the dog. If we try to force an external model onto the church, the result is not only frustration in the ministry of the pastor and the people, but a failure to develop a truly transformational ministry.

The size of the congregation is not an indication of the quality of a church's ministry, nor is it a barometer of the influence it can have in changing people's lives. Any size church—large or small—can have a powerful, transformational ministry. If, however, the purpose of ministry is spiritual transformation, we must have a clear understanding of how to go about achieving the objective, and who we are to influence.

We Are to Transform People by Shepherding Them

One of the pictures used in Scripture to represent the pastoral ministry is that of a shepherd (from which the term *pastor* is derived). This term, used by Paul in Ephesians 4:11, had its roots in the Old Testament understanding of biblical leadership—both in relationship to God and to human leaders. God is depicted as a shepherd who cares for his people, protecting and providing for them (Ps. 23; 28:9; Isa. 40:11). Likewise, kings throughout the agrarian societies of the ancient Near East were regarded as shepherds of their people. Thus, it was natural for the Old Testament writers to refer to God as the shepherd of Israel, and to describe as shepherds the leaders he appointed over Israel.

This imagery finds further expression in Christ's description of his own care for his people. He referred to himself as the Good Shepherd and to his people as his flock. In the early church, the terms *elder* and *overseer* described the position of leadership, but the term *shepherd* was used to describe the function of leadership (1 Peter 5:1–4; Acts 20:28–29).

This picture of pastors as shepherds provides us with a clear perspective of our responsibilities. Rather than being leaders who are visionaries, we are to be shepherds who care for the flock. Glenn Wagner wonders,

> If I came to a new church and showed the people that I was a shepherd, that I cared for them—but did not yet have a vision for them—where would that congregation be in a year? Worst case? I might be pastoring a church of forty or fifty people because my abilities and gifts wouldn't carry me beyond that. But is that so wrong? . . . Doesn't that little church deserve a shepherd who models Christ? On the other hand, where would that church be if I came as a leader with great vision but no shepherd's heart? I think the latter scenario could be more destructive than the former.[4]

Although vision in leadership might be beneficial to ministry, it is not the core of ministry. Instead, pastors are called to provide care for the people. A shepherd is one who understands the people and tailors the ministry to meet their needs.

Effective Shepherds Care Individually for the Sheep

Effectiveness in the pastoral role entails more than overseeing the spiritual well-being of the congregation as a whole. It also involves providing individual care and guidance for everyone in the congregation. The danger is always that we will depersonalize ministry to the point that we are leading the congregation but not ministering to the people. Jesus models individual care by giving personal attention to each person in the body of Christ. He said that a shepherd is one who "calls his own sheep by name" (John 10:3). This implies a personal relationship in which there is intimate knowledge of the special needs and care necessary to bring healing and health to each sheep. Furthermore, writes B. F. Westcott, the word *calls* "expresses personal address rather than general or authoritative invitation."[5] This intimacy is further highlighted by Christ's statement in John 10:14–15: "I know my sheep and my sheep know me—just as the Father knows me and I know the Father." Just as there is personal interaction and involvement between the Father and the Son, so there is personal interaction between Christ and his followers.

As pastors of small churches, we often decry our lack of resources as well as our limitations in the church and in our own giftedness. What we fail to recognize is that we already possess the greatest asset necessary for effective, transformational ministry: a personal knowledge of the people we serve. Because our churches are small, everyone has direct access to us, and we know what is going on in individual lives. We know everyone's strengths and weaknesses, and we know their struggles and triumphs. This knowledge becomes the basis for our effectiveness in ministry. Our interactions with people in the church are personal, specific, and particular, not generic or one-size-fits-all. As we talk to people, we can apply Scripture to specific situations they are facing—not through a formal counseling session but over a cup of coffee or breakfast at a local restaurant.

Effective Shepherds Care for the Needs of the Sheep

When people enter the church, they're not stepping out of a spiritual vacuum, untouched by the prevailing climate of their cultures. Nor do they come to us spiritually whole. Everyone, including ourselves, enters the church spiritually scarred and wounded, damaged by the pains and trials of life. Everyone has been marred by the effects of sin. Like Peter after his denial of Christ, we've all wondered whether God could ever accept and love us again.

Perhaps the greatest tragedy is that often people are unaware of the spiritual scars that plague their lives. The greatest deception of the Evil One is that we are not in desperate need of God's infinite grace and forgiveness. We believe that we are inherently good and acceptable before a righteous God. We've been taught for so long about the importance of having a healthy self-image, we've forgotten that we must think rightly about God before we can think rightly about ourselves. We have forgotten that self-abasement rather than self-elevation is the first step toward spirituality and spiritual wholeness (James 4:10; 1 Peter 5:6).

Consequently, people struggle with their personal identities. They battle depression as they are unable to cope or understand the struggles they face. They harbor anger as the actions of others seem to thwart their own searches for personal fulfillment. The apostle Paul summarizes the reality of many when he writes, "Put to death, therefore, whatever belongs to your earthly nature: sexual immorality, impurity, lust, evil desires and greed, which is idolatry. Because of these, the wrath of God is coming. You used to walk in these ways, in the life you once lived. But now you must rid yourselves of all such things as these: anger, rage, malice, slander, and filthy language from your lips" (Col. 3:5–8). Paul recognized that a dichotomy often remains between the way people live after coming to Christ and the way they ought to live as a result of their new life in Christ. He realized that just because we are called to be like Christ does not mean we will live Christlike lives.

This discrepancy between how we ought to live and how we actually live challenges pastors who seek to shepherd their people. Pastors are the conduit through which God often brings his healing salve to people's spiritual and emotional wounds (Eph. 4:11–16). To do this, we must "feed the sheep"; that is, we must constantly communicate the truth of God in a manner that addresses and brings healing to the spiritual struggles that people face. We bring this healing not through programs but through the proclamation of God's Word.

In the ongoing debate concerning the role and value of psychology to address emotional needs, we mustn't forget that the answer isn't necessarily either/or. Although residents of small and isolated communities may not have ready access to psychological counseling services, when such services are available we should not hesitate in encouraging people to use them, as appropriate and necessary. But pastors of small churches should not forget that, in Scripture, we already have in our possession an invaluable resource by which to restore spiritual and emotional health to people.

This is the role we fulfill as shepherds. We not only mend the broken but also help people find other resources to address their needs. Shepherds also follow up to make sure that people are on their way to emotional and spiritual health. The advantage we have as shepherds of small churches is that we can often identify individuals who are in emotional and spiritual need and we can intervene before their situations degenerate to crises.

Effective Shepherds Protect the Sheep

Spiritual wolves are a constant threat to the sheep. The church operates in a hostile arena where the battles we face are incessant, requiring perpetual vigilance. Consequently, the shepherds must continually be on guard lest the wolves infiltrate and decimate the flocks. Paul warned of this danger in speaking to the leaders of the church at Ephesus (Acts 20:29), and the same threat remains to this day. In our fallen world, false teachers are prevalent, corrupting both doctrine and practical living. They distort the truth of Scripture and the understanding of God and his redemptive plan, and they will corrupt godly behavior in order to prevent people from being transformed into the image of Christ. The challenge we face in the church is not only the preservation of doctrinal integrity, but also the consistent practice of Christ-centered daily living.

One of the traditional strengths of small churches has been their adherence to doctrinal truth. But while preserving orthodox theology through doctrinal purity and diligent activity, they have often fallen prey to the same error found in the church at Ephesus: they have lost their first love. The Ephesians had strongly opposed the heretical theology of the Nicolaitans, but in the process lost connection with their daily relationship with God (Rev. 2:1–7). In our day, small churches have long upheld the doctrines of the church, but at times they have overlooked the greater danger of no longer having a biblical worldview that governs all aspects of life. They are, in effect, living double lives, believing one thing but practicing another. As shepherds of small churches, it is our task not only to correct bad theology but also confront corrupt lifestyles.

To guard against spiritual wolves, we must oppose those who practice heresy as well as those who teach it. In our own ministries, we must avoid the lure of numerical growth at the expense of proclaiming the truth, and the temptation to teach what is popular rather than what is transformational. As leaders who develop close relationships with people in both the church and the community, we must avoid the danger of becoming so focused on relationships that it leads to a compromise in our theology. If, when confronted with theological error, we become silent in order to avoid damaging relationships with people in the community, we are no longer shepherds; we have become as hired hands who abandon the sheep to avoid confronting the wolves (John 10:11–13).

Error infiltrates the church not only from a rebellious, secular culture, however, it also comes from rebels within the church. Paul warns, "Even from your own number men will arise and distort the truth in order to draw away disciples after them" (Acts 20:30). These rebels are individuals who are more concerned about their positions and status in the church than in the health of their congregation families. They promote their own agendas rather than prayerfully seeking God's direction for the church. They reduce the church to a political battleground where they struggle for power and authority.

In the small church, the "tribal chief" is often one who has a deep love for God and a passion for the well-being of the church. However, there are times when their position and authority can become more important to them than what is best for the church. For the pastors of these churches, one of the more difficult tasks they face is confronting the tribal chiefs and loosening authority from them. This should always be done carefully and with an undergirding of prayer, but at times it must be done even at the risk of the pastor's position in the church. Godly shepherds must protect the congregation from anyone, inside or outside the church, who would lead the congregation away from the truth and hamstring the ministry. Confrontation is never easy, and sometimes it might be painful, but it may be necessary in order for us as pastors to be faithful to our calling as shepherds.

Effective Shepherds Sacrifice for the Sheep

Most of us pastors enter the ministry with optimism and a sense of excitement. In our idealism we expect that our congregations will be thrilled by our messages and excited about our programs. With the command of Jesus in our minds, "feed my lambs," we envision a serene pastoral setting where a shepherd lovingly watches over the flock as the little lambs frolic at his feet. It doesn't take long for this idyllic view to be shattered by the pain of rejection, discouragement, and disappointment. Instead of finding a flock of sheep, we wonder if we've been assigned to lead a herd of stubborn mules who possess the viciousness of wolves, the spiritual sensitivity of baboons, and the speed of turtles.

Not only must we deal with broken, imperfect people, but we ourselves are often broken by our own inadequacies, imperfections, and failures. The demands of ministry always exceed our capabilities and resources. We face the difficulty of trying to heal conflicts, deal with emotionally disturbed people—some of whom may be church leaders—and free people who are caught in the snares of sinful behavior. We are confronted by our inadequacies as we counsel couples who have deeply rooted bitterness toward one another, assist parents whose children are rejecting every value and ethos they treasure, and help men and women through the trauma of terminal cancer. In all this we are painfully aware of our own sinfulness and weakness. At times we stand in the pulpit knowing full well that we are not practicing the very message we are preaching. In our despair, we blame our education and complain that the seminary or college did not adequately train us for the problems we face.

The reality is that failure does not lie with seminary or college; no amount of formal training could, in fact, adequately prepare us for the trials we face. What we failed to realize as we entered ministry was that we would have to pay an incredible price to be shepherds and to transform people. When Jeremiah complained to God about the treatment he received at the hands of a wicked people, God reminded him, "If you have raced with men on foot and they have worn you out, how can you compete with horses? If you stumble in safe country, how will you manage in the thickets by the Jordan?" (Jer. 12:5). In other words, "If you can't take the heat, stay out of the kitchen." What we forget is that God called us to transform people through our willingness to sacrifice. Christ himself established the sacrificial pattern: "I am the good shepherd. The good shepherd lays down his life for the sheep" (John

10:11). What distinguishes a genuine shepherd from a hired hand is the degree to which the shepherd places the welfare and well-being of the sheep above his own. The genuine shepherd is willing to pay the price to protect the sheep. Paul recognized the cost of shepherding when he described the trials and struggles he faced in ministry (2 Cor. 4:7–12), but it was a price he was willing to pay: "All this is for your benefit, so that the grace that is reaching more and more people may cause thanksgiving to overflow to the glory of God" (v. 15).

If we desire to change people and transform individuals into disciples of Christ, we must be willing to sacrifice our time, energies, and talents so that others may realize the grace of God operating in their lives. To that end, we must sacrifice our dreams of "success" (i.e., serving larger or growing churches in highly visible locations) to minister to small congregations in isolated communities. We need to recognize that a church of thirty people is just as valuable to God as a church of three thousand. In our market driven, supersize society, it's easy to forget that God values each individual as much as he values the church as a whole. Jesus laid down his life for each and every individual who would become a part of the church. As we follow him and pattern our ministries after his, we should do no less. The power to transform people corresponds to our willingness to sacrifice for them. God did not call us to lives of ease, but to lives of pain, sorrow, and difficulty, so that in the end he might receive the glory as we realize the joy, hope, and peace that transcend our circumstances.

Effective Shepherds Search for the Sheep

The picture that Christ presented of his own ministry was that of a shepherd who leaves the ninety-nine sheep grazing on the hills in order to search diligently for the one wayward sheep (Matt. 18:12–14). It's a wonderful picture of a shepherd carrying his lamb back to the flock. What we as shepherds overlook is that the wayward lamb represents someone who has become ensnared in sin and is in rebellion against God (vv. 15–20). This is not a lamb that merely got lost, but one that deliberately went its own way. In Ezekiel

34:1–10, God indicts the shepherds of Israel who "have not strengthened the weak or healed the sick or bound up the injured," and who "have not brought back the strays or searched for the lost" (v. 4). Shepherding effectively means that we must be diligent in our care for all the people—even those who are in rebellion against God and causing us the most difficulty in ministry. We cannot be satisfied merely to look at the number of people in the pews or how many new individuals have come in the front door. We must also be deeply concerned about the people who leave the church, and we must go out of our way to bring them back into fellowship. Paul writes in 2 Corinthians 11:28–29, "Besides everything else, I face daily the pressure of my concern for all the churches. Who is weak, and I do not feel weak? Who is led into sin, and I do not inwardly burn?" To be effective as shepherds, we cannot allow ourselves to be content when people leave the church, not because their leaving means we've "lost a customer," but because the person has stepped outside of fellowship with God. We are to be willing, diligently and lovingly seeking, to bring them back into a right relationship with God.

Effective leaders—transformational leaders—are committed to leading people to spiritual growth and maturity, not just to imparting knowledge or leading an efficiently run organization. Effective leadership begins when we become involved in the lives of individuals and recognize that transformational ministry is ultimately personal ministry. If we fail to change people, we will never transform the church, for it is only when people are transformed into the character of Christ that the church as a whole will be changed into the character of Christ.

SIX

The Purpose of Leadership, Part 2

Transforming the Church

Can a small church be effective in the midst of a large-church society? The emphasis today is on multi-program churches, with large, celebrative worship, excellent ministries, and a numerically growing congregation. Small churches that do not possess the resources to develop many of the programs and structures suggested by the church-growth models may question their identity and purpose as well as their validity. Small congregations become frustrated, and their frustrated pastors question their own leadership purpose and effectiveness. Can pastors and leaders fulfill their God-ordained purpose in the church even if their congregations are small and remain small? Can a small-church pastor realize God's will while ministering to a small congregation?

To answer these questions, it is necessary to understand the purpose of leadership and the relationship between leaders and the church. The writers of the New Testament did not see a dichotomy between individuals and the community. To be a Christian was to be part of the church community, not through an organizational procedure conducted by the congregation after salvation, but by a supernatural work of the Holy Spirit at the moment of conversion (1 Cor. 12:13). As leaders mentor and disciple the entire congregation—not just individuals—the final test of leadership is found in spiritual influence and purpose, not in results and outward performance.

The priority and purpose of leadership is the same regardless of the size of the congregation. As Henry Blackaby and Richard Blackaby point out, "Spiritual leadership is moving people on to God's agenda."[1] It is important to realize, however, that we cannot "move" people to God's agenda, only the Holy Spirit can accomplish this task. Our responsibility is to continually challenge people to submit to God's agenda and become participants in his plan. As spiritual leaders of a spiritual organism, our task is to continually point the church to God's program. This purpose is not based on resources, whether financial or personnel, or on organizational methodologies, as helpful as they are. This purpose is based on the supernatural empowerment of the Holy Spirit. As small-church pastors, we must be reminded that our leadership is measured in our understanding of God's agenda for the church as revealed in biblical theology, and in the degree to which we have sought to transform the church through our ministry, so that it becomes what God intends it to be (fig. 6.1).

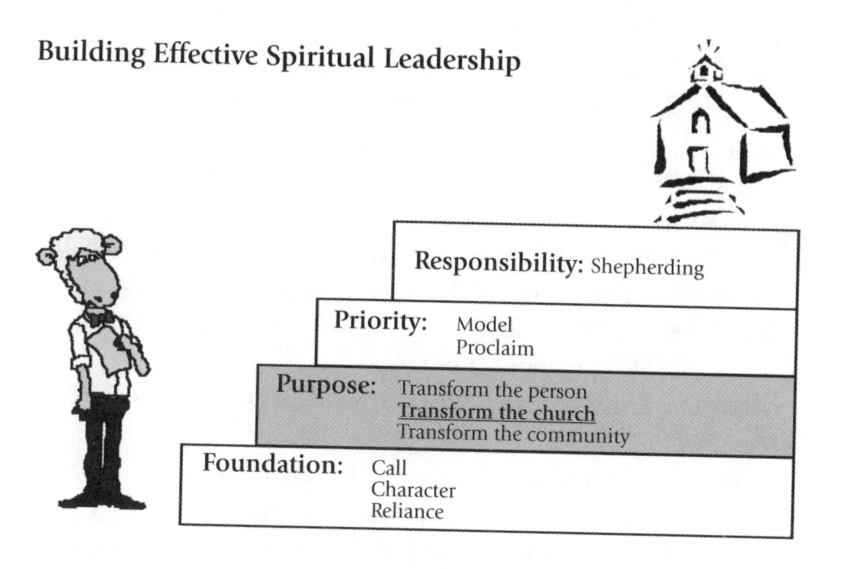

Figure 6.1.

Discovering a Transformational Center

To be a transformational leader in a small church, we must begin with a right understanding of the church and a right understanding of our leadership role.

A Christological Center

Of all the theological studies and disciplines, the study of the church itself typically receives the least amount of attention. Millard Erickson points out, "At no point in the history of Christian thought has the doctrine of the church received the direct and complete attention which other doctrines have received. At the first assembly of the World Council of Churches in Amsterdam in 1948, Father Georges Florovsky claimed that the doctrine of the church had hardly passed its pretheological phase."[2] Little has changed since then. Although it is beyond the scope of this book to attempt such a study of the church, it is important to recognize the center of the church; that is, that which defines its being and governs all its activities. In many churches today, the focus is on the organizational or sociological center of the church. In other words, we view the church in terms of its defining cultural and social dynamics, and we measure the church by its programs, methodologies, and outward growth. In general, large churches tend to focus on organizational dynamics (i.e., its programs, staff, and methodologies), whereas small churches tend to focus on sociological elements (i.e., how the church relates as a community). Thus small churches become defined and governed by the relationships within their congregations. This relational focus is not necessarily bad, but when it becomes the sole defining attribute of the church, then the church has lost its spiritual moorings.

To lead effectively in the church, regardless of the size of the congregation, we as pastors must recognize the true center of the church—and thus the true purpose of the church—which is neither sociological nor organizational. The true center of the church is Christological. Concerning the basis of fellowship, the apostle John writes, "We proclaim to you what we have seen and heard, so that you also may have fellowship with us. And our fellowship is with the Father and with his Son, Jesus Christ. . . . If we walk in the light, as he is in the light, we have fellowship with one another" (1 John 1:3, 7). Our fellowship with Christ and with God the Father becomes, then, the basis of our community relationships within the church. There is, in fact, no church apart from this theological and spiritual relationship with Christ.

Paul also points to the church's Christological center when he writes, "God, who has called [us] into fellowship with his Son Jesus Christ our Lord, is faithful" (1 Cor. 1:9). It is important that we realize that this Christological perspective grew not out of the early formation of the church as it sought to develop its foundations in the community; rather, it stemmed directly from the teaching and mandate of Christ, who gave the church its center and basis for community. In Christ's high priestly prayer, he based the unity of the church on its unity with him. It was this unity that would become a testimony to the world, a testimony of the validity of Christ (John 17:23). A church without a true Christological center to unite and guide everything it does is not a church at all; it is a pseudochurch, pretending to be real but lacking any genuine life. Regardless of a church's size, programs, methodology, or accomplishments, its Christological center is what gives it validity (Matt. 18:20).

Effective leaders are those who continually point the church and all its ministries back to this vital center. In churches large and small, the pastors are effective when Christ remains the center and focus of the church, and when the congregation manifests Christ in all it does, both in the church and in the community.

A Theological Center

The church desperately needs visionary leaders. The type of visionary leader the church needs is vastly different, however, from the type of leader needed in the corporate world. The difficulty is that in modern times the view of the church often has not been theologically defined or driven and this affects the culture's vision of the church. Millard Erickson comments,

> Much of modern theology is less interested in the essence of the church, what it "really is" or "ought to be," than in

> its embodiment, what it concretely is or dynamically is becoming. In a philosophical approach, which is basically deductive and Platonic, one begins by formulating a definition of the ideal church and then moves from this pure, fixed essence to concrete instances, which are but imperfect copies or shadows. In a historical approach, what the church is to be emerges inductively from its engagement with what is—the condition of the world and the problems within it shape what the church is to be.[3]

In determining how the church is to be understood in our contemporary culture, the focus has shifted from a theological starting point—at which Scripture defines the church—to a pragmatic, organizational understanding in which corporate business models and approaches, as well as cultural expectations, define the church. Consequently, the definition of a visionary church leader and what that vision ought to entail differs little from the vision that drives the corporate business world.

From a biblical perspective, however, the church is vastly different from business enterprises and should be viewed differently. Erickson continues, "The church is not very sure of its own doctrine, and consequently may be tempted simply to adopt a view and categories derived from sociological science. As a social institution, the church has aroused the interest of those who study social institutions of various types. They apply to the church the same sort of analysis, which they apply to any social institution, using the same categories. We must be aware that the church is far more than a social institution and therefore must be defined in terms beyond the merely sociological."[4] The church, then, needs leaders who have a clear vision not of what the church should become in terms of growth, programs, and structures. It needs leaders who have a clear vision of what the body of Christ is to be as a spiritual, Christ-centered organism. This vision is to be biblically and theologically determined, not culturally or corporately defined. The church's greatest need today, in terms of leadership, is men and women who have a biblical understanding of what God desires the church to become as both a reflection of the person of Christ and a dynamic influence in the world. The truly visionary leader, then, is the one who has a clear biblical perspective of the church in its ideal and sanctified form, and who is constantly guiding the church in that direction. As such, a leader's success is not determined by what is organizationally successful, but by how much the church is transformed and moving toward the biblical ideal. Vision then becomes the basis by which the leader seeks to influence and transform the church.

The vision that God has revealed in his Word regarding the calling and nature of the church is what gives church leaders passion and commitment in their ministries. Peter Senge points out that what often distinguishes great leaders is "their clarity and persuasiveness of their ideas, the depth of their commitment, and their openness to continually learning more."[5] This commitment and zeal is found in our understanding of God, his activities, and his call to the church. When we have a biblically determined passion for the church, we will significantly influence our congregations and move them forward in their growth as we align our ministries with God's overarching ministry in the church.

Transforming the Church

The writer of Hebrews strikes to the heart of transformational ministry when he warns, "Though by this time you ought to be teachers, you need someone to teach you the elementary truths of God's word all over again. You need milk, not solid food! Anyone who lives on milk, being still an infant, is not acquainted with the teaching about righteousness. But solid food is for the mature, who by constant use have trained themselves to distinguish good from evil" (Heb. 5:12–14). Effective church leadership requires that we as pastors guide our congregations from a state of spiritual infancy and frailty to a position of spiritual maturity and strength. The call to leadership is a call to be transformational in motive, word, and deed.

Leaders Are to Transform the Church into a Spiritual Community

The natural tendency of the church is to drift toward becoming an organizational and sociological entity rather than a living organism in vital relationship with the living God. This drift is seen in the life of Israel in the Old Testament and in the life of the early church in the book of Revelation. Perhaps it was most pronounced during the time of the Protestant Reformation, when a major correction was needed because the church had become steeped in legalism, political domination, and organizational supremacy, and the leaders were more concerned about building and maintaining the structure and programs of the church than they were about the spirituality of the people.

This same natural drift is a danger facing the church today. If the tendency of large churches is to become preoccupied with organizational structure and numerical statistics, the tendency of many small churches is to become overly preoccupied with sociological relationships within the church. Because small churches are often built around strong interpersonal relationships, this fellowship dynamic can begin to dominate decision making and skew the focus of the church. People no longer come to church in search of a meaningful relationship with God but because it fills a vital sociological need. They come because the church is a place where their friends gather to socialize and talk about the events of the week. The result is a church having the form of godliness but denying its power (2 Tim. 3:5), having the outward appearance of a church but lacking the essential element of the church.

When Christ said, "Where two or three come together in my name, there am I with them" (Matt. 18:20), he established the true heart of the church—his vital presence. The church can exist without an external organizational structure, but it cannot exist without the presence of Christ. In its barest form, the church involves two individuals coming together because of their mutual relationship with Christ. This is not to say that structure, organization, and programs are not important to the health of the church. They are. But the organization of the church should never be mistaken for the church itself. The church is ultimately spiritual. Paul reminds his readers that the church consists of individuals who have been united by a common creed—the teaching of the apostles and prophets—and a common foundation—Christ. The church finds its life in its relationship with Christ and its vitality as the dwelling place of God (Eph. 2:19–22). The responsibility of leadership is to continually draw people back to this center. We as church leaders are thus to build a spiritual household, a spiritual kingdom, where the church is in vital relationship with Christ, knowing God and following his will. The church is not a building or an organization; it is a "people called forth by God, incorporated into Christ, and indwelt by the Spirit."[6]

Leaders Are to Transform the Church into a Spiritually Relational Community

Unlike secular organizations, the relational base of the church is spiritual, and this is foundational to its existence. In secular organizations—profit and nonprofit—how people relate to one another is not nearly as important as what they accomplish together. Whether or not they like each other is incidental to how they function as a team and work together. In the church, relationships are spiritually based rather than sociologically based, and thus are essential to the church's existence. To be a part of a spiritually relational community, one must first be in relationship to God. When God told the people of Israel that he would be their God and they would be his people, he established a covenant community based on relationship. The glue that bound the people together was their relationship with God. This promise was not that the people would know about God, but that they would experience him as their God.[7]

This same theme is carried over into the New Testament. When Christ prays, "That they may know you, the only true God, and Jesus Christ, whom you have sent" (John 17:3), he is not praying that we as believers would have a cognitive understanding of God, or that we would know about him. Rather he is praying that we would experience the full reality of God in our total humanity—intellect, emotion, and will—and in our total experience of life. When someone enters the church for the first time, he or she may know about God—knowledge much of which is often distorted—but have no experience with God. He or she may have a cognitive understanding but not an experiential/relational understanding. New converts do not know what it is like to walk daily with God, to have God guide and direct their daily lives. They do not know what it means to live out one's life in the center of God's will and rest in that center. Our task as leaders is to lead people into this spiritual and relational transformation.

Because believers have a spiritual relationship with God, we are called to live also in spiritual relationship with every other person in the body of Christ. We're called not to mere tolerance of one another but to mutual care, concern, and involvement. We cannot claim to be in fellowship with the body of Christ if we harbor hostility—whether active or passive—toward another member of the church family.

Aside from spiritual relationships, human interpersonal relationships are the greatest strength of a small church—but also its greatest weakness. Although many small churches are like families in which members genuinely care for and about one another, this same relational closeness can make the church a closed community that is difficult for new people to join. Newcomers who do not follow unwritten but well-established sociological or cultural norms are viewed with suspicion. New members are often relegated to "ministries" such as taking the offering but are not given positions of authority or influence. Leadership positions are reserved for "old timers," and positions of influence are often determined by bloodlines rather than spiritual maturity.

Further, small churches can confuse friendship with fellowship. Friendship is when individuals are bonded together because of sociological connections. They enjoy being with one another because of shared experiences and interests. Fellowship, although related to friendship, is much deeper. The bond of fellowship is spiritual rather than sociological. Fellowship is when two or more individuals form a bond with the purpose of challenging and assisting one another toward spiritual maturity (Heb. 10:25). The role of leadership in transforming a small church into a relational community is to help people move from friendship to fellowship, so that their relationships will make a significant difference in their spiritual growth.

Leaders Are to Transform the Church into a Serving Community

"Who is going to harm you if you are eager to do good?" the apostle Peter asks (1 Peter 3:13). A closer examination of this verse reveals several striking insights.

First, the word translated *eager* is the same term from which is derived the word *zealot*. It speaks of one who is a fanatic. The word *zealot* typically conjures up images of wide-eyed fanatics who are passionately crazy for their cause. It is interesting, therefore, to note that the writers of the New Testament use this term on three occasions to describe what should be the Christian's attitude toward a life of service. In addition to Peter's use of the word in 1 Peter 3:13, Paul exhorts believers in 1 Corinthians 14:12 to be "fanatical" in our search for spiritual gifts; and in Titus 2:14, he states that Jesus has "purified for himself a people that are his very own, 'zealots working to do good'" (author's translation). A healthy church is one that is passionate and fanatical about practicing good.

Second, Peter uses a third-class conditional construction, which implies that this zeal is not yet a reality but should be. In other words, we humans are not naturally fanatical about doing good, but we believers must develop this characteristic. If we want to be like Christ, zealous to do good, we must manifest an outward orientation, and "in humility consider others better than [our]selves," and "look not only to [our] own interests, but also to the interests of others" (Phil. 2:3–4). This attitude, though, does not come naturally to us in our fallen condition. Instead, we focus on our own wants and needs. Take, for example, the way in which some people select a church. If they feel that a particular congregation does not "minister to my needs," they'll leave in search of one that will.

This same mind-set shows itself in a different way in many small churches. Although the members often have a strong sense of loyalty to the church, and thus are not likely to move on, they can tend to become focused on the internal needs of the congregation and ignore or shun people outside the church, especially those whose lifestyles and attitudes are not consistent with those of the people within the congregation. A small church can easily become a closed community that ministers effectively to itself, but not to those outside. Most small churches struggle, too, with limited finances and personnel; consequently, they tend to focus their programs and ministries on members of the church rather than on services for people outside the church. As a result, the church becomes ingrown. Our responsibility as leaders is to move the church away from being an egocentric organization and toward becoming a serving community. When Christ called the church to "go into all the world," he gave a mandate for service.

Third, Peter issues his call to be "fanatical about doing good" in the context of responding evangelistically to people who are actively opposing the church. If the church is to reach others with the gospel, it must be through service and in spite of adversity.

Transforming the church into a serving community begins with raising people's awareness of the spiritual, physical, and emotional needs of people outside the church. Too often, churches remain oblivious to the social problems such as poverty, crime, substance abuse, and so forth in their communities. Churches with a mindset to serve will seek to minister to those needs rather than condemn the people plagued by the problems. When a church becomes active in serving the community, it will begin to have a transformational effect on the community.

Transforming the church into a serving community, however, involves training and equipping people for ministry. In Ephesians 4:12, an oft-quoted passage, Paul reminds us that our task as pastors is "to prepare God's people for works of service." For Paul, preparation for service was an essential ingredient in effective leadership, "so that the body of Christ may be built up" and dynamically changed. When a congregation becomes a serving church, the people are built up in their faith and knowledge of the Son of God.

Leaders Are to Transform the Church into a Creedal Community

Although theology and doctrine are much maligned in many churches today, they are no less important than ever. The absence of sound theological doctrine will, in fact, ultimately undermine the health and vitality of the church. Because the church is not a social organization but a spiritual entity, what it believes about God and about God's activity in the world is central to what it becomes as a spiritual body. Paul warns Timothy that "the time will come when men will not put up with sound doctrine" (2 Tim. 4:3). For Paul, the first step in spiritual apostasy and moral compromise was the loss of a sound theology.

The church's creeds, that is, what the church believes, are its lifeblood. Creeds govern our actions as believers, stimulate our conduct, guide our church's programs. The task of leadership is to develop within the church a creedal community where theology is lived out, not just taught. We as leaders must teach and demonstrate a sound, biblical understanding of who God is and what he does in redemptive history. This then becomes the foundation for the lives of each individual—including ours as pastors—within our communities. In our creedal communities, our theology of God determines our perspective on every circumstance in our lives. We must become communities where our decisions align with the nature and will of God, not with what brings the most pleasure, which is the world's standard. In our creedal communities, right thinking about God is formulated in order for us to think rightly about ourselves and the world in which we live. In our creedal communities, truth governs our understanding of experience rather than experience governing our understanding of truth. It is lamentable that in the church today so many pastors are no longer teaching sound theology. People by and large have become theologically illiterate. When this happens, moral and spiritual compromise are inevitable.

Leaders Are to Transform the Church into a Missional Community

Small churches continually struggle to get by with limited resources. As small-church leaders, we dream of a day when millions of dollars would be available to develop our facilities; when we'd have enough people to staff multilevel, specialized programs; when the worship leader can go on vacation and a number of other people would be available to ably fill in. Until that day, however, which likely will never come, we struggle to maximize outdated facilities, and scramble to find leaders to staff basic programs, often asking people to perform two or three jobs. We strain to keep the church afloat, both financially and functionally, in a cultural environment where the church is increasingly viewed with indifference at best, if not open hostility. As Robin Trebilcock points out in *The Small Church at Large,* "In a hostile climate there is a natural tendency [in the church] toward defensive, conservative values. This response is a capitulation to the difficulties. The pioneer wagons in the defensive circle against the marauding tribes are stuck; even though within the circle there will be feelings of normalcy and safety."[8] As churches struggle to exist, it's tempting to want to "circle the wagons and hope to survive." Circling the wagons, though, is the one thing that will ensure a church's demise.

God did not call the church, after all, merely to "survive"; and a missional church is one that realizes as much. Rather, God called the church to take the message of the gospel to a spiritually hungry world. A dynamic church will be oriented toward missions, which includes the local community and embraces the world. A vibrant church will place its organizational survival on the line in order to reach out to the world with the redemptive truth of Christ. But because small churches often struggle to stay afloat, they can easily become so preoccupied with survival that they lose their missional focus, and thus assure their own demise. What Christ said of individuals, however, may equally be said of the aggregate church: "Whoever wants to save his life will lose it, but whoever loses his life for me will find it" (Matt. 16:25). But it must not be forgotten that God himself is the one responsible for the church's survival (1 Cor. 3:6–7; Mark 4:26–29). Like the apostles, churches must be willing to die for the sake of the gospel. But when churches are more concerned about saving their organization and protecting their facilities than they are about building the universal body of Christ, they have signed their own death warrants.

Our task as leaders is to continually bring the church back to its missional responsibility. We must constantly challenge the church to risk everything for the cause of redeeming the world. When a church goes all out in pursuit of its God-given mission to reach the world, that church discovers the dynamics of true spiritual health: God sustains and provides when the outlook is bleakest.

The call to leadership is a call to transform the church into a genuine reflection of the bride of Christ. It is not a call to maintain status quo or keep the church afloat. As leaders, we can ill afford to sit back, passive and indifferent to the mission of the church. We must be active and purposeful in our efforts to transform the church into the biblical model of what God intends for it to be.

Discovering the Transformational Process

How to be a transformational leader in the context of the church today remains a perplexing challenge for those of us in ministry. The mistake in the past has been thinking that we can transform the church through vision casting, mission statements, program growth, and organizational structures. Although each of these elements has its place, we have often overlooked the first most important element—the biblical mandate to preach the Word. When Paul encountered a spiritually unhealthy church, he did not develop a five-step renewal program or recast the church's organizational vision. Instead, he confronted the issues through the development of a biblical theology.

The church at Corinth was in deep spiritual trouble. It had allowed sin to go unchecked, it was devastated by divisions and immorality, and it refused to submit to authority. But rather than coming in and reorganizing the church, Paul made it clear that the key to spiritual transformation was the preaching of the Scriptures (1 Cor. 2:1–5). From Paul's perspective, only the life-giving message of Christ, demonstrated in the powerful work of the Holy Spirit, could provide the basis for transforming the church from spiritual sickness to spiritual and organizational health. Likewise, when Paul wrote to Timothy, who also was ministering in a problematic church, he did not advise him about programs and methodology but about the necessity of biblical preaching.

The church does not need preachers who enable people to feel good emotionally or even spiritually; the church needs preachers who seek to transform people spiritually through the communication of God's

Word. We as preachers, then, cannot forget that the primary means by which the Holy Spirit brings about change in a person's core being is through the presentation of Scripture (Heb. 4:12). Programs, although helpful, are only beneficial to the extent that they help us communicate biblical truth. Any program that does not have as its core purpose the presentation and proclamation of the Scriptures is a social program, not a spiritual transformational program. This is not to say that every program or gathering of the church must include a sermon. But everything we do should be designed to build relationships with people in order to foster communication and receptivity to the message.

Second, in addition to proclaiming biblical truth, transformational leaders must model a biblically consistent lifestyle. The congregation will follow what the leaders do, not only what they say. To develop a transformational serving church, we must continually model biblical humility and service, exercising our gifts, talents, and abilities for the encouragement and growth of others rather than for ourselves. Thus, we must model godly and loving relationships with everyone in the congregation. Further, if the church is going to reach out to the community at large, the leaders must embrace people who do not "fit" into the church's subculture.

Third, leaders must be devoted to prayer and seeking God's direction. Because transformation is ultimately the work of the Holy Spirit in the life of a congregation; prayer is foundational for change. Without prayer, any change will be superficial and temporary. Spiritual leaders must remain committed to prayer as well as to seeking God's empowerment and direction in transforming their congregations.

Finally, leaders must examine every ministry and program and evaluate them according to the church's biblical and spiritual mandates. Are these programs contributing to the spiritual transformation of the congregation? Although programs are never an end in themselves, and no program can guarantee spiritual transformation, they nevertheless are an important part of the process by which transformation occurs. Consequently, to bring lasting and significant change to the church, we must assess every program in light of its contribution to the transformational process.

SEVEN

The Purpose of Leadership, Part 3

Transforming the Community

The church was never intended to simply exist within a community, isolated and without impact. Christ clarified the role of the church when he asked his Father not to remove the church from the world but to protect it from evil influences (John 17:15). The church, then, is to be a visible and real presence in the community. We have a responsibility to people outside the church to proclaim and demonstrate the gospel of Jesus Christ. We are not merely to enter the secular world to do business and earn a living and then retreat into the church community for "spiritual work." In Scripture, there is no dichotomy between "secular" and "sacred." We are to engage with the community at every level.

This call to engage with the community provides the greatest opportunity for a small church to reach its maximum potential. But it also exposes the church's greatest weakness. Especially in small communities, where churches still play an important role in community life, we as small churches can often have an influence that far exceeds our size. Pastors are still seen as spiritual leaders in the church and social leaders in the community. In times of crisis, small communities look to pastors and churches for assistance. In rural communities—where there is often a significant shortage of social programs and resources that assist the poor, provide help in times of natural disaster, and deal with social and economic pressures—the church can play a vital role. At this critical juncture, however, many of us small churches have become so preoccupied with not being "of the world" that we are no longer "in the world." In our quest to avoid moral compromise, we have so isolated ourselves that we have lost all moral influence in our communities.

This isolation and lack of influence is exacerbated by the lack of resources available to most small churches. Even if we desire to engage with the community, we often resist using our resources to do so for fear of threatening our very existence. We're often reluctant, for example, to allow the community to use our church buildings during the week for fear that the wear and tear will exceed our resources to maintain the facilities. But in our fear of risking the future of the church, we undermine the very future we seek to preserve. If small churches are to survive, we must seek to be integral to our communities and to influence our communities. "If we today stress the spiritual aspect of the gospel without the social," writes Os Guinness, "we lose all relevance in modern society. But if we stress the social without the spiritual, we lose our reality altogether."[1]

Understanding Our Prophetic Role

Although it is true that the pastor/teacher gift is distinct from that of the prophet, pastors nevertheless have a prophetic role to play. Too often, we as pastors focus on the predictive nature of prophecy and overlook its primary role in Scripture—that of addressing current social and spiritual issues through the proclamation of Scripture. In *The Prophets of Israel,* Leon Woods describes the prophets' role:

> The manner of speaking by the prophet may be best characterized as *preaching*. Here the idea of preaching is used as over against the idea of teaching. In teaching, one addresses primarily the mind of the hearer, while in preaching he addresses the emotion and will. The interest of teaching is to impart information; the interest of preaching is to stir reaction and response. The work of Israel's priests was to do the former; that of the prophets was to do the latter. . . . Though

> the prophets did predict at times, as God gave them this kind of information, the greater part of their declarative ministry was in preaching to the people of their own time. They were really much like preachers today, urging people to live in a manner pleasing to God. They used prediction in their preaching only on occasion, whenever it was necessary to impart a message God wanted given.[2]

The prophets challenged people with the truth, in order to transform individuals and the entire community. Often, they focused their message on the leaders, because they realized that the health of a community depends on its leadership.

As our society continues to grapple with increasingly complex moral issues, our spiritual leaders must address these issues through the prophetic voice of the Word of God. If we are to be effective leaders in the church, our leadership must extend beyond the church walls where we seek opportunities to become advocates for the socially disenfranchised in the community at large. Our communities need biblical leaders who are able to relate Scripture to life, and who are willing to challenge the community to address moral and social ills with biblical solutions.

As preachers, we must be brokers of truth to the world. God has something to say to our society, and he has chosen us to be his mouthpieces. The basis of this prophetic role stems from the very nature of God's Word and the order that God has established in creation. Wisdom literature recognizes that God's morality is absolute and the universe is governed by these moral absolutes. The strength of a nation is not determined by its military might or economic strength, but by its adherence to the moral absolutes established by God. Although we are not called to establish a theocracy in governmental politics, we are called to influence our society so that people adhere to the moral laws that form the foundation of society.[3] Our task is not to save the country or make it a "Christian nation," but we are to be involved in our society in order to encourage an environment where the gospel may be readily proclaimed (1 Tim. 2:2).

Being Salt in the Earth

Christ, in admonishing and preparing his disciples for ministry, instilled in them that they were the salt of the earth (Matt. 5:13). Concerning Christ's statement in the Sermon on the Mount, D. A. Carson writes, "Implicitly he is saying that apart from his disciples the world turns ever more rotten: Christians have the effect of delaying moral and spiritual putrefaction."[4] The church is to do more than coexist with secular culture; it is to have a positive moral influence on society at large. We members of the church community do this as we become positive models for the world to both examine and follow. This influence goes beyond the message we proclaim to include how we act and react to the world in which we live. Paul states that we are to "be wise in the way you act toward outsiders" (Col. 4:5). That is, we as a church are to be both interactive yet cautious so that we are not negatively influenced, responding both in word and deed in a way that reveals Christ to the world. When we as individual believers work diligently at our jobs, are honest in our business dealings, and positive in our attitudes toward the government, we have a positive influence on others. When the world mistreats us and we respond with kindness and blessing, we have a positive influence on others (1 Cor. 4:12–13). In the process of living our daily lives in accordance with Scripture, we develop a positive reputation with people outside the church (1 Tim. 3:7).

The Role of the Church: Transforming the Community

The church has always had and will continue to have a significant effect on the moral, social, and spiritual framework of the surrounding community (fig. 7.1). This is especially true in rural society. Sociologists would say that people do not inherit a specific culture or knowledge of cultural expectations. Rather, we as people learn our culture and its expectations through the process of socialization, which "takes place within the social organizations closest to us—the family, school, and church. Other institutions, including community organizations such as civic groups or social clubs, play a lesser role. Collectively, the social organizations through which culture is transmitted are called *agents of culture.*"[5] As an agent of culture, the church "can preserve the past or work toward change; which course they take depends on the character of their relationship with the community."[6]

The church shapes its surrounding communities by instilling moral and ethical standards that govern people inside the church and significantly influence people outside the church. It has this influence because it is a social center as well as a spiritual center for people inside the church and in the community at large.[7] The church, then, shapes society by providing for the community's social and economic needs. In many small communities, the church is a primary resource for providing assistance to people who face emotional and economic crises. "Community solutions, when they do occur," writes sociologist Cornelia Flora, "are often the task of voluntary associations rather than a responsibility of local government. This puts a heavy burden on rural churches, for example, to organize meals-on-wheels programs and care for the elderly or to provide the kinds of food, clothing, and shelter for the poor, both those who live in the community and those who pass through."[8]

Building Effective Spiritual Leadership

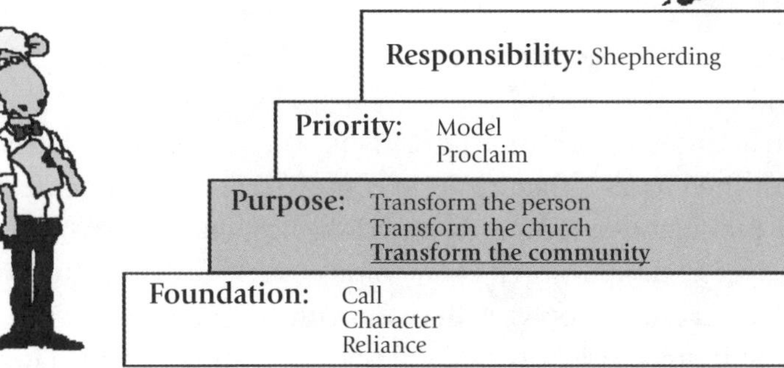

Figure 7.1.

Because churches play a significant role in rural communities, pastors are often viewed as community leaders, as well. To have an influence, however, we as church leaders must recognize the importance of contributing to the life of the community. Pastors who isolate themselves and only serve the church will become isolated from the community and not respected by it. Pastors who become involved in activities outside the church, such as volunteering in community service organizations, will be respected and will have a greater voice in the cultural formation of the community. Volunteering with the fire department, serving as the chaplain for the local sheriff's office, or becoming part of the PTA are more than avenues by which a pastor can build relationships outside the church and in the community. They are also the means by which a pastor gains respect and contributes to the well-being of the whole community.

Transforming the Community by Addressing Moral Issues

North American society is facing a moral crisis. Like many of the great societies throughout history, our culture is on the verge of abandoning—and in many ways, in fact, already has—the moral absolutes that have served as its foundation. When these moral absolutes are abandoned, social collapse is inevitable. We are already feeling the tremors of a moral earthquake that threatens the stability of our nation. Like the Canaanites of old, we have become worshipers of the goddess of sexuality with her temple prostitutes (actresses and actors whose sexuality is displayed in the guise of artistic expression) and legitimatized immorality. The worship of sex is paraded in the movies, on television and radio, in magazines—not only *Playboy* and the like but also in many women's magazines and *Sports Illustrated,* with its annual swimsuit edition. No corner of society has been left untouched by its influence. Even commercials for all kinds of nonsexy products like computers and chewing gum use sexuality as the basis for their appeal. The scandalous use of sex to recruit college athletes is only an outgrowth of our cultural preoccupation.

The tremors are also shaking the foundations of our families. With the redefinition of "family" to include all sorts of nontraditional living arrangements, the government-authorized issue of marriage certificates to gay and lesbian couples, and the continuing epidemic of divorce, families are under assault, both inside and outside the church. A pastor providing premarital counseling can no longer assume that the couple is not having premarital sex, even if both individuals have been raised in the church. Most children no longer grow up in homes where both parents are present. The result is a generation that has no idea what a normal family environment is like.

Even more frightening are the moral questions being raised in the medical community. From stem cell research to cloning, science has opened up a Pandora's box of moral issues that make the abortion debate pale in comparison. No longer is it a question of when a baby becomes a viable living person, but now the question is can we determine what kind of person that baby will be? While the medical world scrambles to find its moral center, many churches blissfully go about their business of having potlucks and boxing up care packages for missionaries. Leonard Sweet warns, "A flood tide of a revolution is cutting its swath across our world and is gathering prodigious momentum."[9] If churches do not start providing answers quickly—and we can all be thankful that many are—we will lose our moral voice in a world crying out for moral guidelines.

As the moral foundation of society crumbles, substance abuse and crime continue to rise. Long regarded as inner-city problems, they are rural problems as well. In largely rural states such as Kansas, Montana, Nebraska, and Wyoming, the per capita crime rate exceeds that of urbanized states such as New York and New Jersey. Because drug and alcohol abuse have long been thought to be urban problems, people sometimes move from urban centers to rural areas in order to remove their children from these pressures. In recent years, though, substance abuse in rural areas has grown to equal the rate in urban areas. In one national study, the amount of drinking by rural high school students exceeded that of their urban counterparts.[10] The church, though, has failed to adequately address these tragic problems. Cornelia Flora writes, "Rural ministers [who] report attempts to have prevention programs through the churches are met with resistance by the congregations. In some areas, church members feel that people should not drink at all. Drinking is viewed as an individual moral problem rather than a response to societal pressures. Thus, there are no societal solutions, only individual ones."[11] In an area where the church has answers, it has largely remained silent.

One of the critical roles that pastors and churches can play in a community is to provide the foundation for making moral decisions. In smaller communities, we pastors often develop personal relationships with people such as doctors, law enforcement officials, and politicians, who influence the community at large. Often, these individuals will come to our churches, and we can help them formulate a biblical mind-set and demonstrate to them the morality of Scripture. Although we recognize that we cannot save people through political agendas, we can influence our culture by maintaining a voice in the community. In small communities, we can serve on committees that oversee school policies. We can be a part of the local social services, providing oversight for food banks and other such programs. To do this, however, we must build relationships with people in the community. By becoming involved in community service organizations, we become a part of the community rather than just "the pastor of the corner church."

Transforming the Community by Addressing Social Issues

In many smaller, geographically isolated communities, the church can and should address social issues such as poverty. In recent decades, rural areas have seen a steady decline in income and continue to lag substantially behind urban areas. The agricultural economy, once the backbone of rural areas, has become increasingly more volatile, putting pressure on families and churches as people struggle to stay solvent. Although the 1990s saw a decrease of the poverty rate in rural areas (from 17.1 percent to 14.6 percent), more than four hundred non-metro counties (out of a total of 2,308) have poverty rates over 20 percent and are classified as chronically impoverished.[12] Blacks, Hispanics, and Native Americans are especially plagued by chronic poverty.

This economic disintegration has resulted in an increase in stress on community social structures. Because rural areas typically lack the social structures and economic assistance programs available in urban areas, the focus for helping people in need shifts to the church to provide financial assistance.

A second social issue confronting the rural church is an increase in the number of elderly people, who also increasingly tend to be poor. The Economic Research Service reports that rural areas have a higher proportion of older persons in their total population than urban areas.[13] Because rural areas also lack resources (transportation, medical, social) to provide for the needs of the aged, these people often turn to the church for help.

A third growing social issue is the migration of Hispanics into rural areas. This influx of new immigrants increases economic pressures and ethnic tensions as Hispanics "take jobs away from" other residents. These same tensions are found on Indian reservations as tribes seek to regain the autonomy promised to them under various treaties. Furthermore, as tribes gain more economic power and influence through gaming and other tribal programs, it increases the tension between Native Americans and other residents.

Rural areas also suffer from an outward migration of young people. Although rural populations have increased overall in recent decades, they have consistently decreased in the twenty- to twenty-nine-year-old age group. As young people graduate from college, they no longer see the family farm or rural economy as a basis for economic stability. Instead, they migrate to urban areas in search of higher paying jobs and better career opportunities. The result is not only the graying of many rural communities but also the graying of rural churches. Sunday school programs continue to decline as there are fewer children in rural communities. The church then becomes discouraged because things are not like they used to be.

These social problems are issues to which the church cannot afford to turn a blind eye. They are, in fact, the very issues addressed in the Old Testament. As pastors, we must speak up for the socially disenfranchised. We must do more than isolate ourselves and our churches from these issues. We must take the lead in dealing with poverty, meeting people's daily needs, and developing economic strategies to get them out of their impoverished situations. As Walter Kaiser points out, "Poverty is systemic and continues in the face of the best efforts of the best government to eradicate it. This can be no reason for a person or a government to excuse itself, but it does call for a constant 'open hand' (Deut. 15:11) on the part of those who have been provided with more than the needy."[14]

It is easy to become judgmental of people on welfare. Many of us in the church tend to be critical because we view the problems of welfare recipients as the self-induced result of drug and alcohol abuse and promiscuous sexual activity. Even if it is true that many people in need have contributed to their own problems, we should not become callused toward them. Instead, we must help them with their physical needs as we address the spiritual needs that are at the root of their problems. To our shame, it is far too easy to be cynical rather than caring, to be judgmental rather then redemptive. But Christ, our perfect model, was most compassionate to social outcasts, to those whom the rest of the society scorned. Christ demonstrated compassion without judgment so that these people were drawn to him and found him to be a place of refuge. This should also be true of the church, the body of Christ today. Wherever poverty exists, whether in the inner city or out in the country, the church must be active in ministering to the needs of people.

Transforming the Community by Addressing Spiritual Needs

The goal of transforming morally and socially the communities at large that surround our churches is ultimately spiritual and redemptive rather than sociological or cultural. In the past, however, the church has fallen naturally into two errors. The first is the error of social action without proclamation of the gospel. The second is proclamation of the gospel with indifference toward social, economic, and emotional needs.

For many Christians, social action has replaced the gospel as the center of the church's involvement in the community. The church feeds the poor, works for the disenfranchised, and advocates for the downtrodden, all the while allowing people to travel the road to eternal destruction without warning them of their impending doom.

On the other side of the coin, the church warns people of their impending doom but does nothing to provide food for the hungry. As the example of Christ so vividly reveals, social action and proclamation of the gospel are not two separate works; they are intricately interwoven into one desirable goal, which is to save people from the punishment of sin and build the kingdom of God. Consequently, small churches must look beyond their own four walls and minister to the physical, emotional, and spiritual needs of people in their communities while confronting sin and proclaiming the good news of salvation in Jesus Christ.

The challenge of spiritually affecting rural communities is not a matter of marketing. In suburban areas, where churches are plentiful and often unnoticed, marketing strategies can be an effective tool to raise the church's visibility in the community and connect it with people. Marketing is not as effective in rural areas, where people have long been aware of the church's existence. The task here is not to raise people's awareness so they can decide to come to church, but to reach people who have already made a decision not to attend. To accomplish this objective, the church must minister to the needs of people in the community by becoming involved in the growth and well-being of the community. To gain a hearing, we the church must earn the right to be heard by becoming involved in the community.

Positive relationships open the door for the church to minister to people's spiritual needs. How the church relates to the community determines how receptive the community will be to the church's message. The amount of influence we as pastors personally have is directly related to the perception the community has of us. Paul recognizes the importance of reputation when he writes, "Be wise in the way you act toward outsiders; make the most of every opportunity. Let your conversation be always full of grace, seasoned with salt, so that you may know how to answer everyone" (Col. 4:5). This is especially true for pastors. If we desire to influence our society, we must be aware of the importance of how we act. When Paul reminds Timothy of the qualifications of those who aspire to leadership in the church, he writes, "He must also have a good reputation with outsiders, so that he will not fall into disgrace and into the devil's trap" (1 Tim. 3:7). Without a positive reputation, a pastor becomes open to accusation—whether true or not—which undermines that pastor's ministry and undercuts his testimony. Thus, to influence others for the cause of Christ, pastors must build positive relationships in the community.

Relationships start with meeting people. In our age of technology and mass marketing, we pastors often overlook the importance of personal visitation. Darius Salter, in his discussion of evangelism in a technological age, points out, "It is still understood by most non-Christians that the gathered people who meet at specific times and places, whom the Bible designates as the *ecclesia,* is the primary source for spiritual food."[15] If non-Christians still look to the local church for their spiritual food, they look to the pastor as one who conveys truth. We cannot, however, expect people to come to us to find the answers to their spiritual questions. We must go to them. Kennon Callahan rightly states, "Mission movements visit as naturally as people breathe, as regularly as the sun rises and sets. With mission movements, visiting with community persons is in the very fabric of their being. It is through visiting that they reach out in sharing and shepherding ways to those in community."[16]

Visitation is the means, too, by which we as pastors can build relationships in the community and reveal the reality of Christ. Visitation, however, has become a lost art because many pastors misunderstand what it is. Visitation is more than knocking on doors, which has become less effective because people lead increasingly busy lives and are often not home. Visitation can occur at a local restaurant, where the locals congregate to share a cup of coffee. Visitation includes going to basketball games, sitting next to unchurched people, and cheering on the local team. Visitation means helping ranchers with their branding, playing in the town softball league, and volunteering to be a chaperone on the school's field trips. Visitation means being where the people are.

Callahan expands our understanding of visitation: "I encourage you to visit with persons in the same ways people ordinarily visit with one another. In everyday life, people are in contact with one another in many ways. . . . Look anew at how people in your community share and visit with one another. These will likely be the most effective ways for you to be in contact with persons in the name of Christ."[17] We as pastors can transform a community only when we are in the community and become a part of the community. Otherwise, we will remain outsiders with limited influence.

Building these positive relationships means contributing to the community. Especially in rural areas, people expect the local pastor to do more than provide care for the church. They look to us for care and assistance in times of trials, and for aid in times of natural disasters. They expect us to be involved in social programs for drug prevention, economic assistance, and crisis counseling. Thus, before our message will be heard in the community, the people must see our message lived out in our lives. Transformational ministry begins, therefore, when we become contributors to the social well-being of the community, then we earn positions of influence. It takes time, sincerity, and effort to move from being an outsider to being a person of influence in a community. Building respect doesn't happen overnight; it often takes years. One reason why the church has failed to remain influential is because pastors don't stay very long in small churches before moving on. Consequently, they never become part of their communities, and thus have little voice.

A second way in which we can minister to the spiritual needs of our communities is through technology. Technology is never a substitute for personal contact, however, and studies indicate that it has little direct influence on bringing people to a point of conversion. Yes, writes Darius Salter, "Electronic evangelism holds the potential of serving as a contributing force in the discipling of people who are either in a pre- or post-conversion religious experience." Further, he writes, "There will always be the liability that haunts all mass evangelism—an instantaneous mentality that often skirts the intricacies of Christian nature. In the meantime, it will serve as a supplement, for better or worse, to the myriad forms of evangelistic endeavor that have been practiced down through the centuries."[18] Sponsoring, too, a five-minute devotional broadcast on the local radio station not only raises the visibility of the church in the community but can also be an avenue for a pastor to minister to people's needs by giving biblical answers to the struggles they face. A Web page, which is often available free of charge by a local provider, can be an effective ministry tool. People can be drawn to the Web site to find information about community events and school activities, and then can also find a daily devotional, perhaps, and information about the church.

Third, we can minister to our communities' spiritual well-being by training our congregations to serve. Often, in rural communities, people tend to separate their daily lives from their ministry. They see ministry as something they do on Sunday and often in conjunction with a particular program of the church. They view the daily witness and ministry of the church as the pastor's responsibility. Because of the close-knit nature of a small church, people have a high degree of sensitivity and concern for each others' needs. Although this is commendable and important, it can cause the church to become so inwardly focused that it loses sight of the needs of people in the community at large. The church becomes self-centered in its thinking and ministry. If we want to have a transformational influence in our communities, we must teach people to look outside the four walls of the church building to identify the needs of others in the community.

Having trained people to identify needs, the church must also equip people to meet those needs by strengthening and utilizing their spiritual gifts. For example, a person who has the gift of teaching may teach English as a Second Language (ESL) classes during the week, in addition to teaching Sunday school. A gifted mechanic might set aside one Saturday a month to do automobile maintenance for widows or single moms. Retired folks who are still active and able to drive might offer to transport elderly people to doctor's appointments. There is no shortage of needs in most communities. What is lacking is people's awareness that they can utilize their talents, gifts, and abilities to help people and in the process reveal the reality of Christ.

Finally, pastors must lead the church in providing resources and assistance. This may include providing biblical training to help people share their faith and answer spiritual questions. It may involve helping people to find the right training materials for Bible studies, discipleship training, or other activities. Pastors can also help to allocate financial and equipment resources for ministry to people outside the congregation. For this to occur, churches must be committed to the mandate of reaching their communities. The pastor's task is to remain committed to the outreach of the church. Kevin Ruffcorn writes, "If a congregation is to be evangelistic, it is necessary for the pastor to carry the vision of evangelism in his or her own ministry and share this vision with the congregation."[19] If pastors lack the passion and commitment for transforming their communities, so will their people.

To be effective in reaching and changing our communities, we must become involved. If we isolate ourselves, we isolate the gospel. As we become involved in our communities, we gain a hearing for the presentation of the gospel.

EIGHT

The Priority of Leadership, Part 1

Being a Model

It doesn't take long in ministry for the excitement and joy to wear off as days are filled with the tasks of sermon preparation, visitation, and counseling. What starts out as a pastor's dream of church growth and dynamic ministries soon bogs down in the reality of the continual struggle to maintain the church's present ministries. Even if the congregation remains enthusiastic about their pastor's ministry, as leaders we become discouraged when the hoped-for growth does not happen and people leave the church because they are moving to different communities for greater employment opportunities. This discouragement is compounded when others leave the church to attend larger churches in neighboring communities because the larger churches "have more ministries for our needs."

Consequently, we read books about church growth and developing effective visions. We implement a number of different ideas that we think will enable the church to more effectively reach the community. Often, however, even after the congregation has put forth significant effort, nothing seems to work. Our discouragement is further compounded by pastors conferences and seminars where it is implied that numerical growth is a sign of God's blessing because the church is doing what God desires. Pastors conferences thus become a further source of discouragement. Although we enjoy the fellowship with other pastors, we feel intimidated as we hear stories about the growth of other congregations and how God has blessed their ministries, and we wonder why God is not blessing ours.

The problem lies not in our lack of effort or our spiritual sensitivity to God, but in our misguided approach to ministry. Because we have overcomplicated ministry with programs and methodology, vision development, and organizational management, we have become confused about the biblical priority of ministry. Scripture, however, gives a different set of priorities: setting a godly example for others and proclaiming the message of God's Word. If we are to have a transformational influence, we must keep the proclamation of Scripture and sound doctrine at the core of our ministries (1 Tim. 4:15–16; 2 Tim. 4:1–5). Paul writes in 1 Timothy 4:6, "If you point these things out to the brothers, you will be a good minister of Christ, brought up in the truths of the faith and of the good teaching that you have followed." The word *good* here refers to that which is healthy and useful, "the total state of soundness, health, wholeness and order, whether in external appearance or internal disposition."[1] An effective ministry is one that is healthy in the sight of God, in which the pastor is faithfully applying biblical truth to the life and conduct of the congregation. An effective ministry is not necessarily "seeker sensitive" or "market driven," as helpful as those strategies might be; rather, an effective ministry is first and foremost biblically centered. When we focus on proclamation of the Word and personal character, we become more free in ministry, because the focus is off our own talents, skills, and abilities and onto God's work accomplished through us.

The Living Word: Christ, Our Model

When Christ came to earth, he came with the purpose of being our substitute and taking upon himself the wrath of God so that it might be diverted from us in order that we might experience God's grace. Although this was his primary purpose, he also came to provide for us a model of how to live. As the living Word of God, he was both the revelation of God's nature and the one who showed us perfectly how to live before God. He provided a living example of how the written Word is to be applied and implemented in the daily affairs of life. This is the same task to which we as pastors have been called. As we follow Christ's example, we become living examples for others to emulate (1 Cor. 11:1).

When Paul writes to Timothy concerning the priority of Timothy's ministry, he reminds him to "set an example for the believers" (1 Tim. 4:12). Timothy faced a difficult challenge in ministry when the people questioned the validity of his leadership because of his age and inexperience. Paul does not tell Timothy to work harder or to exert his authority by demanding that the people follow his vision. Instead, Paul challenges him to be an example for others to follow. The phrase *set an example* is a command, implying that it is not a sidelight of ministry but an ongoing, central task. The word *example* is a term from which we derive our English word *type;* it refers to the imprint an object leaves behind when pressed against a softer substance, such as the impression of a seal on melted wax.[2] "[The] thought here is not that of an ideal, but of a model that makes an impression because God has molded it, and this is effective through faith. Word and deed bear witness to the life of faith that summons to faith and is grasped by faith. The more life is molded by the word, the more it becomes a typos."[3]

In today's world, moral, ethical, and spiritual confusion permeate our culture, both in the community and in the church. People

Building Effective Spiritual Leadership

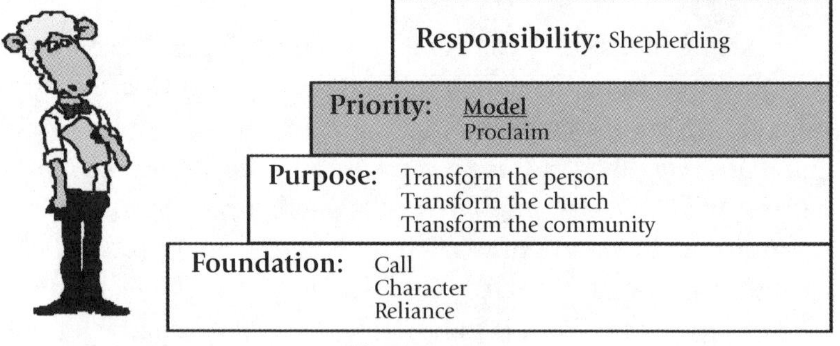

Figure 8.1.

today struggle not only with understanding what is biblical truth, but also how it is to affect their daily lives. As emphasized by figure 8.1, the task of leadership is to bring reality to faith, to provide a living model of what it means to be a disciple of Christ. Not only are we church leaders to develop and teach a biblical worldview, but we must also demonstrate, by how we live our lives, how that worldview shapes the choices we make, the attitudes we manifest, and the responses we give to the pressures we face. As Eugene Peterson says, we are to be "spiritual directors." This, however, is often not accomplished through formal leadership channels. "The things that we do when we don't think we are doing anything significant might make the most difference," Peterson writes. "By its very nature—obscure, everyday, low profile, non-crisis—this is the work for which we need the most encouragement if we are to keep it at the center of our awareness and practice. It is in fact the work for which we get the least encouragement, for it is always being pushed to the sidelines by the hustling, career-development mentality of our peers and by the hurrying, stimulus-hunger demands of our parishioners."[4]

How we as pastors live—our being—has a far greater effect on our ministry than the tasks that we do. Yet we continually face the pressure of doing rather than being. Often we become so involved in "doing ministry" that people are never given the opportunity to see us simply *be*—and thus we have little impact. Unless we model for others what it means to live Christianly in a pagan world, our lives will never effectively shape the lives of others. This is why Paul, in each of his letters to pastors, places so much emphasis on modeling rather than performing (1 Tim. 4:12; Titus 2:7; see also 1 Peter 5:3). When our lives become signets that leave an imprint on our congregations, our congregations become signets that leave an imprint on other people (1 Thess. 1:7). For this to happen, however, we must live in such a way that our lives affect how others live.

A common complaint among small-church pastors is that people know us too intimately and examine our lives too closely; yet the very thing we resent is actually the basis of the strength of our ministries. The reason we have such an impact on people is because they get to know us. They see how we respond to the struggle of sin. They see how we react when we are frustrated and discouraged. They can watch how we respond to a rebellious teenager. They see us with all our warts and blemishes, but they also see how faith in God and reliance on Scripture can be applied in a fallen world.

Personal Character: The Basis of Ministry

"Follow my example," Paul writes, "as I follow the example of Christ" (1 Cor. 11:1). In order for ministers to be effective in ministry we must first be transformed by our own relationship to Christ. Before we can be models for others to follow, we must make sure we are following the right model ourselves. This means being character driven. It means allowing God to transform our lives so that we can be used to transform others' lives. Transformational ministry does not spring up from the level of our education, our talents and abilities, or our accomplishments. It flows from the spiritual vitality of our personal encounters with the living God.

As pastors of small churches, we often sense our inadequacies in ministry. When we compare ourselves to multitalented individuals who have achieved significant accomplishments, we feel not only that we have failed, but also that we are incapable to handle the demands of ministry. When we see our churches fail to grow numerically, it only further confirms in our thinking that we are unfit for ministry. It is a profound loss when some pastors leave the ministry because of these feelings, and it is wearying for others who continue on, continually plagued by doubt and discouragement. Pastoring small churches stretches us beyond our capabilities, and we do not have the luxury of multiple staff members to buttress our weaknesses and perform the ministries that we are untrained to accomplish.

The problem is not with us or with the ministry. The problem is our perception and understanding of what it takes to be effective in ministry. "Character is infinitely more strategic to effectiveness than credentials," writes Joseph Stowell.

> For instance, character is universally obtainable. Credentials are attainable by only a gifted few. Character develops a legacy that will cast its shadow over generations to come.

> Credentials are quickly forgotten. Character is transferable from the leader to those whom he's leading. Credentials are not transferable. Character is a means to glorify Christ through our lives, since it is His character, the expression of our belief in Him, that is reflected through our lives. Character makes a point about Him. Credentials make a point about us. Character is both magnetic and motivating. As others see a growing deepening sense of goodness in our lives, they will be drawn to us and feel stimulated to follow suit in their lives. Credentials set a distance between us and others and may discourage others who can't attain, or incite jealousy and covetousness. Character is what we will be held accountable for. Credentials won't count on the day that we stand before Him. Character is only forged through a growing, sincere relationship to Christ. Credentials can be gotten quite apart from Christ. Character is deepened and developed in crisis. Character has value in a crisis. Credentials are of little avail when the chips are down. Credentials set us on a pedestal while character erects a platform from which we can minister.[5]

No amount of education or accomplishments can overcome a weak or flawed character. Because our ministry as pastors flows from our characters, we are called to a higher standard in obedience to the moral, ethical, and spiritual mandates of Scripture. The character and godliness of the people in the pews will not exceed the godliness of the leadership. This point was illustrated repeatedly in the life of Israel. When the kings and the priests were devoted to serving God, revival penetrated the land as people turned away from the idolatry that continually plagued the nation. When, however, the kings rebelled against God and were bent on pursing their own agendas, the people reverted to paganism and idolatry.

The focus on character creates a tension for pastors in our lives and ministries. While we preach the perfect standard of Christ and strive to model that standard, we never measure up to it perfectly. Instead, even as we preach righteousness, we are painfully aware of our own sinfulness and inadequacies. The problem is, we and the people we serve often harbor a mistaken perception that spiritual maturity should equal perfection. We echo the cry of Paul in concluding that we are completely wretched (Rom. 7:14–24). Yet the same Paul unabashedly called on people to follow his example. His boldness did not come from confidence in his own abilities, but from a deep awareness of his dependence on God and on the power and grace of God's work in his life (Phil. 3:7–11; 4:13). To be a godly example does not require absolute perfection in our conduct and attitudes; it requires only that we be in subjection to Christ, recognizing our complete dependence on God for all things. This necessity for dependence is why our fixation with methodology becomes a false foundation for ministry, because it removes God from the equation and places human wisdom at the center.

Developing Personal Character

As much as we as ministers preach about developing personal character, we often neglect it in our own lives. In small churches we often become so involved in "doing ministry" that we fail to take care of our own spiritual health. As Steve Bierly points out, "In the small church, if you are to keep growing spiritually and professionally, you're going to have to be a self-starter. If you won't take care of you, no one else will."[6] This need is further compounded by the isolation that many small church pastors experience, especially in rural areas. Because we have little contact with other pastors, we often do not have a support network available to provide spiritual encouragement and accountability. We have no one challenging us in our spiritual growth and well-being, no one with whom we can discuss our spiritual struggles and temptations. Consequently, we must learn to pastor ourselves.[7]

The first element necessary for the development of personal character is the development of personal study of Scripture for the purpose of personal growth, not just professional preparation. Because we pastors have so many demands on our time and energy, it's easy to start regarding sermon preparation as our "personal devotions." The problem is that we no longer personalize our faith, asking what

God is saying to *us* in his Word. Instead, we approach the Bible only to discover what God is saying to everyone else. Before long, even as we give solid nutrition to our congregations, we become spiritually anemic. Paul continually challenged Timothy to take care of his own spiritual well-being. Likewise, we are to train ourselves to be godly and to persevere in our doctrine and our lives (1 Tim. 4:7, 16). When Paul gave his final challenge to the leaders in Ephesus, he challenged them to "keep watch over yourselves" (Acts 20:28). The most effective messages are not the ones in which we have used perfect and entertaining illustrations. Neither are they the ones in which we have perfectly expounded the meaning of the text, although doing so is critical. Rather, the most effective messages are the ones in which we have seen ourselves in the pages of Scripture and have allowed God's Word to change us first. Then we can not only bring relevant application to the people, but they can see a living model of how to apply the passage to themselves. It is when our congregations see God's truth lived out in our lives that they become challenged and encouraged to apply God's truth to their own lives.

A second element necessary for the development of personal character is an active prayer life. It is ironic that the one activity that Christ made central to his life (Matt. 26:36–46; Luke 5:16; 6:12) is the one activity we often struggle with the most. The apostles, in fulfilling their ministry, made prayer central to their work (Acts 6:4). For them, their chief business was spending time in the study of Scriptures and in prayer. Yet these are the very things that are pushed out of busy pastors' schedules as we strive to fulfill the demands of program development, counseling, and visitation. While serving in a small church, it is easy to become so involved in the activities of ministry that we neglect the most important elements of ministry. It is all too easy to allow prayer to become a fire alarm, placed on the wall for use only in extreme emergencies. What we must recognize is that prayer is both an action and an attitude. It is an action in that it requires deliberate and planned activity. Thus, we are to consciously set aside time to pray. Although the amount of time spent in prayer will vary by individual, the action itself should not be overlooked. Prayer is also an attitude by which we continually recognize and live in our complete dependence on God. When Paul exhorts us to pray continually, he is reminding us that we are to live every moment, and face every decision, with the awareness that we are dependent on God's wisdom, grace, and guidance.

A third element of developing character is the cultivation of accountable relationships. Commitment without accountability is an aspiration without fulfillment. If we are committed to spiritual growth, but not accountable to others for that growth, then it will always remain a dream rather than a reality. Scripture reminds us that we need accountability to grow (Eccl. 4:9–10; Heb. 10:24–25; James 5:16). It is a serious oversight, though, that while preaching the importance of accountability we often neglect it ourselves. H. B. London Jr. and Neil Wiseman report that seventy percent of pastors do not have someone they consider a close friend, someone in whom they can confide.[8] The results are devastating, both emotionally and spiritually, as isolated pastors become vulnerable to temptation, discouragement, and spiritual defeat. The paradox for pastors of relationally focused small churches is that their defining characteristic is the very thing that leads to isolation of the pastor. We often fall prey to the misconception that if we develop a close relationship with someone in the church we are showing favoritism. In small churches, each member expects and wants to have a personal relationship with the pastor. They all want a pastor who spends time with them and is their personal friend. If the pastor spends time with only one family or develops a close relationship with someone, others feel slighted. Consequently, as the pastor strives to be everyone's friend, he becomes so stretched thin relationally that he does not develop a close friendship with anyone.

Another reason why small-church pastors become relationally isolated is because we fear that people will see us with all our faults and think less of us. We fear that our ministry will be jeopardized if we get off the pedestal by being real with people and allowing them to see our struggles and weaknesses. In order to counter the fishbowl effect and protect our privacy, we prevent ourselves from growing close to anyone in the church. This fear of vulnerability is compounded when people are ready to condemn us for the slightest mistake.

A further reason we struggle with isolation is because we often are viewed as outsiders in our own churches. Even though the people love us as their pastors, they may regard us as strangers because we do not share their cultural background and perspectives. This perspective is reinforced by every short-term pastor who passes through town. Consequently, some people develop the unconscious mind-set that the pastor is someone who comes from the outside and will soon be leaving, and so they have no real desire to get close to the pastor. The result is that pastors become further isolated from the people in their congregations.

If we pastors are to maintain our spiritual growth, we must develop supportive, accountable relationships with people in the church. Like anyone else, we need close friendships in order to be emotionally and spiritually healthy. Otherwise, the attrition rate among pastors will continue to be a significant problem for small churches. Experience has shown that nobody else in the church will take the initiative to look after our emotional and spiritual health. Thus, we must do so ourselves by becoming vitally connected within our churches.

A fourth element necessary for the development of personal character is intellectual growth. Just as our people need a steady diet of spiritual and biblical instruction, so do we. But because we are the primary teachers in our congregations, we often do not have the opportunity ourselves to be taught by others. This deficiency is further compounded by our isolation from other pastors and groups with whom we could have academic and spiritual dialogue and interaction. Nevertheless, even though we're isolated, we can still be instructed by maintaining a steady diet of reading. Studying what others have written enables us to be taught without having to leave our offices.

Intellectual growth is not a luxury in ministry; it is critical to our spiritual fitness for ministry. Recognizing our need to grow theologically and biblically is crucial, both for our health and for the health of our congregations. We need to be aware of current theological trends and issues. We must continually expand our understanding of the unifying message of Scripture by reading various books on biblical theology. We need to sharpen our exegetical skills so that we are able to "correctly handle the word of truth" (2 Tim. 2:15). In order to do so, we periodically need to read books that address hermeneutical and exegetical issues so that our interpretive skills will be sharpened and we might correctly understand and apply Scripture. It is essential that we read books dealing, too, with leadership in the church. Every week we face issues that challenge our ability to lead the church. Seminary education, as beneficial as it is, cannot fully prepare us for all the issues confronting us in ministry. If it did, it would require decades of study rather than a three-year program. Thus, we need to supplement our seminary education by reading books on management, conflict resolution, program development, and ministry priorities. Also, we should study issues of practical theology, such as marriage, discipleship, family, and other topics relevant to the needs and issues we face in life.

To be effective in ministry, the growth we inspire in the members of our congregations must spring forth from the personal growth we experience. Without personal growth, we will eventually suffer spiritual burnout. Ministry may never become easy, and we may never feel fully equipped and adequate to the demands and responsibilities of our calling, but we can establish a firm foundation for continued effectiveness by growing intellectually and pursuing a godly character. We can lead our people only to where we ourselves are going.

Being a Model

Transformational ministry is not built on programs or methods; it grows naturally from lives that are worthy of emulation. Our greatest opportunity for influence is the example we set of how to live a godly life. Whether or not people respond immediately to our message, "they will know that a prophet has been among them" (Ezek. 2:5) when we have faithfully communicated God's message and have modeled a godly lifestyle.

Ezekiel had a transformational influence not because he developed elaborate programs but because he was faithful to God's calling in his life and his message. When Paul wrote to Timothy exhorting him to be an example (1 Tim. 4:12), his challenge was about more than just ministry. It was a summation of everything Paul had taught Timothy about character-based, transformational ministry.

We Are to Model Godly Speech

What we as pastors say to people has a significant effect on their spiritual growth. As pastors of small churches, we must realize that what we say during the week, and how we say it, has as much impact as what we say from the pulpit on Sunday. What we say, and to whom, can make or break us in ministry. If we inadvertently betray a confidence, we can lose the trust of the entire congregation. If we misrepresent the truth in order to look better, we will lose people's respect. The grapevine operates very efficiently in a small church. Thus, a wise pastor will continually guard his speech.

We must be especially careful when talking about our churches. When we get together with other pastors, for example, do our conversations center on what is wrong with the church and how unspiritual the people are? If we are not careful, we can become cynical, blaming the congregation for every problem. Although there is certainly a need and a place for seeking advice from other ministers and sharing burdens for mutual support, we can easily become critical and judgmental and develop an us-versus-them mentality. When this happens, our conversations become destructive and discouraging, no longer supportive and beneficial. Pastors who continually criticize the church become critical of the church. We can become congregational gossips, sharing struggles and weaknesses with people who are not directly part of the solution. Controlling our speech involves protecting our congregations and believing in our congregations.

We Are to Model Right Values

When Paul states that we are to be models of life, the term he uses can refer to both positive and negative conduct. The determining factor for conduct is the ethical value system that governs a person's behavior.[9] To live rightly, we must avoid reverting back to secular modes of conduct (2 Peter 2:17–22), becoming slack in our attitudes toward sin so that we no longer call it what it is. Because we are constantly under pressure to promote numerical growth and attract new people, we can be tempted to compromise the moral teaching of Scripture. Alcoholism, for example, becomes a disease rather than a sinful attempt to find happiness apart from God. Immorality becomes an alternate lifestyle rather than a perversion. In our quest to keep our message positive and palatable, we water down the truth. The result is that we preach a God of love, but no longer a God of absolute holiness who demands uncompromised perfection.

The second pitfall in the pathway to formulating right values is the snare of legalism. In the quest to avoid the errors of compromise and liberalism (or libertarianism), many small churches have fallen prey to legalism. Because liberalism is perceived as having no boundaries, the small church builds a fence around the law, focusing on outward performance rather than inward transformation. Legalism places law above grace, demanding that people adhere to an external code of conduct in order to develop inward righteousness that will transform external conduct. As a result, the culture of a small church replaces Scripture as the arbiter of proper behavior, and people who do not adhere to the church's code of conduct are ostracized. An environmental activist with long hair, for example, might—regardless of his spiritual maturity—be shunned in a ranch community because he does not adhere to the cultural expectations of an agrarian culture where people are land-use proponents. His external behavior is thus deemed more important than his inward transformation. On the other hand, people who adhere to these external cultural expectations are viewed as righteous. Our responsibility as pastors is to lead people to inward change that results in a deep love for God and an intense desire to obey and serve him. Although a church should be culturally sensitive and adaptive, we should never be so culturally driven that spirituality is defined by adherence to cultural norms rather than biblical mandates. We as pastors must enable people to see that biblical faith is greater than the culture in which we live and that biblical truth must govern all expressions of faith, even those within a specific cultural setting.

To model right values, we pastors must focus on godliness and Christlikeness, and we must show others how to live under the control of the Holy Spirit. People are not only looking for faith, they are looking for someone to show them how to live out their faith in the daily affairs of life. Therefore, we must demonstrate right priorities, beginning with right attitudes of service. As disciples of Christ, we are to live lives of service before God, not for personal gain but for the benefit and spiritual health of others (1 Peter 4:10). In short, we must practice what we preach. We often decry pastors who serve for selfish motives, yet we fall prey to the same mind-set ourselves. We might preach against consumerism in our sermons, but what does our attitude toward finances reveal about what we really think?

One of the pressures that pastors face in small church ministries is the struggle to survive financially. Many small churches have difficulty finding and keeping pastors because of the candidates' financial expectations, and pastors often leave in search of greater financial security. Patricia Chang reports that the difficulty of finding pastors for small churches today is not the result of a shortage of available pastors, but a shortage of pastors willing to pastor small or rural ministries where salaries as well as job opportunities for spouses are limited.[10] We pastors may preach one thing but model another in the way we select and evaluate ministry opportunities. Pastoring a small church is not easy, and it often requires financial sacrifice. To remain in a small church, a pastor must often be willing to live on a limited income. Doing so can cause financial stress, leading to bitterness toward the congregation because they maintain a higher standard of living than the pastor. Furthermore, people often expect a pastor's standard of living to be equivalent to that of the lowest-paid working-class family.

Peter, too, challenges elders to serve the church because of a divine calling, not because of financial remuneration (1 Peter 5:2).

Paul states, too, that spiritual overseers are not to be motivated by money (1 Tim. 3:3). Pastors are to be examples of moral and ethical conduct, placing our trust and confidence in God for our daily necessities (1 Tim. 6:17). To avoid compromising our ministries, we must learn to trust God and to be content with his daily provision (1 Tim. 6:5–10). If we seek to break the hold that materialism has on our culture, we must set an example of godly living.

Second, we model godly values by giving proper priority to our families. It is easy to place the demands of ministry above the needs of our families. George Barna reports that more than 50 percent of pastors believe that their vocation has been difficult on their families.[11] Rather than blame our congregations or the ministry, we must recognize that the fault lies in our own desire to be successful. But as Paul writes in 1 Timothy 3:5, "If anyone does not know how to manage his own family, how can he take care of God's church?" We must recognize that our ministry begins at home; the home is, in a sense, a microchurch. If we cannot provide effective spiritual leadership to this microchurch, how can we expect to lead the larger church family?

Because in a small church our families are placed under the microscope of people's expectations, we must protect our families by making sure that the task of ministry does not override our responsibilities at home. We must communicate to the church that our children are normal kids with normal struggles and challenges, not supersaints.

Because in a small church the pastor is expected to be at every committee meeting, we must schedule meetings judiciously to avoid being away from home every night of the week. If we allow the schedule to run us, rather than the other way around, we not only hurt our families directly but we also model a devalued perspective of our families.

People will still call and expect our time at all hours of the day, and we must learn to distinguish what truly requires immediate attention and what can be dealt with later. We should put our family times on our calendars and tell people we have a previous commitment during those times. By our actions we communicate to our families that they are more important to us than our ministry.

We Are to Model Positive Relationships

We live in a world of broken and fractured relationships, both inside and outside the church. Adult children are estranged from their parents. Married couples are on the brink of divorce. Parents struggle to relate to their children, and vice versa. People in the church are bitter about decisions that have been made. It is little wonder that Paul calls upon Timothy to be a model of love. In the Old Testament, the word for love *(hesed)* emphasizes loyalty and faithfulness, based on a commitment and a covenant. On the basis of this covenant, God acts to save his people from disaster and oppression. When *hesed* is used to describe the love between two individuals, the emphasis is on loyalty stemming from a covenantal or familial root.

The New Testament term *agape* also emphasizes a deep commitment that leads to action. Joseph Stowell provides an excellent summary: "This agape love is the kind of love that chooses to understand the needs of another and then responds to those needs by expending available resources to meet those needs."[12] *Agape* love is critical in ministry.

As pastors, we committed ourselves to the universal church when we entered the ministry. That commitment, however, often doesn't extend to the local churches in which we serve. Small churches by and large suffer a revolving door mentality in the parsonage, as pastors stop by for a few years until something bigger and better comes along. We tell our congregations to be committed to the church, yet we fail to model that same commitment. If we are to effectively demonstrate love, we must also demonstrate our commitment to the local church. This means we no longer view a small church ministry as a temporary assignment until an opportunity arises to pastor a larger church. It means we are willing to stay until God makes it clear that our ministry is completed. Without this commitment to loyalty, pastors will never fully be trusted and accepted. As David Hansen points out, "When a church and a pastor do not bond, the church cannot grow—in numbers, in commitment to one another and to God, to mission, to worship, and to a deeper spirituality. The simple reason is that all growth involves change and risk, which causes most individuals and all congregations profound anxiety and threatens to keep us from taking the steps to growth."[13] If our churches are to mature under our leadership, we must verbalize and demonstrate our loyalty. Only when our congregations feel secure in our commitment will we be able to lead them toward necessary and lasting spiritual growth.

We Are to Model a Dependence on God

Faith means taking God at his word. It involves both the act of belief and the object of belief. It is placing one's focus on the character of God and his Word, and then acting on that knowledge. Faith is both the foundation for salvation and the foundation for life. We are saved by faith and we are to live by faith (Rom. 1:17; 2 Cor. 5:7). Living by faith means responding to every situation in a way that is consistent with the attributes of God and what he has promised in his Word.

We, as leaders, striving to model a dependent faith, must set an example in three strategic areas:

1. *Demonstrating faith that God will provide for all our physical, emotional, and spiritual needs.* As pastors it's easy for us to place our confidence and security in the church. The danger is that we will start making decisions based on what brings security rather than on what is right. We must always remember that we stand under God's authority and that ultimately we work for God, not for the people in the church. There are times when it is necessary for us to take a stand for what is biblically correct, even though it might be unpopular and threaten our financial security. Paul warned Timothy about the dangers of being controlled by popularity and appeasing people rather than pleasing God (2 Tim. 4:2–5). At times, we may need to lovingly rebuke an individual according to proper church discipline, even when it results in a negative reaction (1 Cor. 4:1–5).

2. *Manifesting faith in the face of problems and difficulties.* We often pay an enormous emotional and spiritual price as we minister to the needs of others. We risk being misunderstood and unjustly criticized. We encounter rejection because of our faith. We struggle for answers as we help people overcome the trauma of an infant's death or a young mother's cancer. We feel inadequate as we face conflicts in the church that have been festering for years. These challenges are further compounded by the financial struggles that face most small churches. But faith trusts that God is working in every situation to accomplish his purpose. Not that we blindly hope everything will turn out in the end, but we are confident because God is faithful and sovereign. Setting an example of faith means we do not complain about the circumstances, problems, and difficulties we encounter in life and in ministry. We do not complain about our limited resources. Rather we rejoice in God's activity, seeking to respond in a way that honors God and reflects his character.
3. *Trusting God for the future and for the church's activities.* We can easily become discouraged when membership declines, as people move out of the community, and the programs that we established fail to bring in new people. But we must minister and live by faith, setting an example for our congregations to follow. We cannot challenge the church to be people of faith if we ourselves are not living by faith, trusting God rather than our own ability to develop programs and establish the right methodology to accomplish the results. Faith means trusting God for all things in every area of life and ministry. God in turn will utilize all things for our spiritual maturation, for the benefit of his church, and for his glory.

We Are to Model Moral Integrity

The last quality mentioned by Paul in 1 Timothy 4:12 is moral purity, which includes sexual purity but involves much more as well. Moral purity is a manner of conduct consistent with the moral and ethical demands of a holy and just God. The foundation for this command is Christ, who is pure and untainted by sin (1 John 3:3). Moral purity encompasses all actions, behaviors, and attitudes that govern a person's moral, ethical, and spiritual conduct. Our power and authority as church leaders spring forth not from our talents and qualifications. If we compromise truth, or manipulate people to achieve our own purposes, we will lose credibility. Although we can never be perfect, we should model consistency in growth. Because we are called to be spiritual leaders, not merely organizational managers, it is not enough that we preach and plan well. We must also live well, developing an inward godliness that manifests itself in a godly lifestyle.

Being an Effective Model

To "set an example for the believers in speech, in life, in love, in faith and in purity," we pastors must recognize the importance of character-based ministry. Who we are is far more important to the well-being of our small churches than what we have accomplished. Paul himself based his ministry on the pursuit of Christ and his character, not on his own credentials, as significant as they were (Phil. 3:1–11). People will always follow a talented, charismatic leader, but that doesn't necessarily mean they have been led in becoming transformed. At the end of our lives, we will be evaluated not by what we have accomplished in building impressive ministries, but by who we are. In being a model for transformation we can serve our small churches joyfully with our hearts set on God.

Being a model involves realizing the value of relationships. Unless we're close to people, we cannot imprint our lives on them. Although our small churches face many struggles and shortcomings, our greatest strength is the closeness of our relationships with everyone in the congregation, including the children. We should never underestimate or devalue the importance and significance of this intimacy. Nor should we resent the lack of privacy that often accompanies close relationships in a small church.

When everyone wants to know, and often does know, everything about our lives and our families' lives, we can be tempted to resist the transparency that ministry brings. Yet this transparency is the very foundation of our ministry. Because we live transparent lives and people can see our strengths and weaknesses, they can also see how we deal with pressures, temptations, and struggles. We are living models to our congregations of how to live in an imperfect world with a fallen, sin-plagued nature. Our faith gives reality to their faith, not in the sterile atmosphere of a church service but in the nitty-gritty details of daily life. They see us not as supersaints who are perfect but as common, average people who face the same struggles they face. It is our transparency that gives us credibility in our preaching and teaching.

"While it's easy to resent the visibility factor of shepherding," writes Joseph Stowell, "it is important for us to remember that it is our visibility that gives us viability in the work. Were God to grant us our wish to be invisible, we might be happier, but there would be no ministry."[14] This is especially true in a small church. Without transparency, we pastors never become part of the congregation and the community; we remain as outsiders. Although it is often difficult to cross the divide between being an outsider and being an accepted part of the community, we'll never make it if we don't willingly allow people to see us for who we really are.

Finally, if we are to be effective models of Christlikeness for people to follow, we must maintain our spiritual growth and consistency. A moral or spiritual failure can ruin a ministry. Although we recognize that we'll never attain perfection in this lifetime (Rom. 7:14–25; Phil. 3:12–14), we continually strive for spiritual maturity and consistency. We seek to live lives that are above reproach and not open to accusation (1 Tim. 3:2). The test of character is not just what we do at any given moment, but what we do over the long haul of life. Still, we can undermine years of ministry and modeling by a moment of moral failure, which is why we are held to a higher standard (1 Tim. 3:1–7; James 3:1).

The call to ministry is a call to be a living model for others to follow. It is a call to live our faith in such a way that it provides a living picture of what it means to be like Christ. This is the calling of all pastors, but in a small church the picture is magnified. Little wonder, then, that the position of small-church pastor holds such significance.

NINE

The Priority of Leadership, Part 2

Preaching the Word

A perusal of books on church leadership shows a common focus on a number of different tasks—program development, vision casting, organizational leadership, and goal setting. Strangely absent from much of the discussion is the role of preaching in the context of leadership. This is quite unlike what is found in the New Testament, where proclamation of the Scriptures is not a sideline of leadership but the very center of our calling as pastors. Paul felt so strongly about this, in one of his letters to Timothy he declared that Timothy's ministry would stand or fall on how effective he was in proclaiming the Word of God to meet the spiritual needs of people (1 Tim. 4:1–8). Whenever the New Testament describes the activities of the early church leaders, it always revolves around the proclamation of truth to the situations of the day. The call to leadership, then, is a call to proclaim God's Word to meet situations in our day.

Students of culture are continually announcing the drastic and universal changes occurring in our society. Just when we think we are beginning to understand our culture, another megashift brings a new set of norms and values that drastically affect our lifestyles and how we do church.[1] Technology, for instance, has come up with solutions to make our lives easier and safer, but has brought as well an entirely new range of threats that shake our world. Nor did the end of the Cold War end the nuclear threat; it simply transferred it into the hands of radical terrorists who would welcome the opportunity to die for their cause. Bioterrorism, once the stuff of sci-fi movies, is now a real threat to our security. Even the borders of the United States, once a haven from international conflict, are no longer safe.

The problems facing modern society are not just technological and political. The breakdown of the family has spawned an entire generation that grew up without the presence of both parents in the home. For them, a normal family has a single parent—or four. The decline of the family coincides with a rapid shift in moral and ethical standards. What was once immoral and indecent is now considered normal. This has led to a hotly debated and emotionally charged cultural war sweeping across the nation as traditional values clash with modern liberalities.[2] Those who strive to maintain a high moral standard are labeled as radical extremists and bigots with no love for their fellow human beings.

Rural America is now at odds with urban America over environmental concerns. In many ways, rural people are the new minority. Policies governing how they live are being established by people who have little understanding or concern about the effect those policies have on the families that populate the countryside. Family farms are being forced out of business because of policies passed by largely urban policy makers, further compounding the economic crisis facing rural America, where more and more people are living below the poverty line.

In our cities and suburbs, the rising crime rate, shifts in demographics, and economic downturns have a tragic affect on people at all levels of society. In two-parent homes, both partners now work, not in order to acquire luxuries but to afford basic necessities. The cost of housing, insurance, and transportation is forcing many people to work longer hours, and the issues related to latchkey kids continue to be a significant concern.

In the midst of all this, pastors are called upon to provide prophetic insight that gives people answers. In the growing turmoil of ethical, moral, and societal shifts, people need absolute solutions that transcend culture and provide a moral anchor. It is to this role that pastors are called. Biblical leadership is not about organization—although it involves administration; it is not about planning—although it requires goals and direction; it is not about programs—although it includes program development. Biblical leadership is about speaking the Word of God to contemporary society.

The Priority of Preaching

People in the church today do not need another business leader who maintains the organization and plans corporate strategies. They need someone who can speak prophetically to the issues of the day. The single most important task we perform as pastors, that which determines our success as leaders, is, in fact, our proclamation of biblical truth (fig. 9.1). If the goal of leadership is to transform people, and if transformation comes through the truth of the Word of God, then the task of leadership is the faithful proclamation of that truth. Pastoral leadership is all about helping people think and act biblically. We may not be strong visionaries, we not may possess dynamic personalities or draw people easily to our ideas, we may not be great program developers, but if we faithfully proclaim God's Word so that people are transformed, then we are effective leaders.

Building Effective Spiritual Leadership

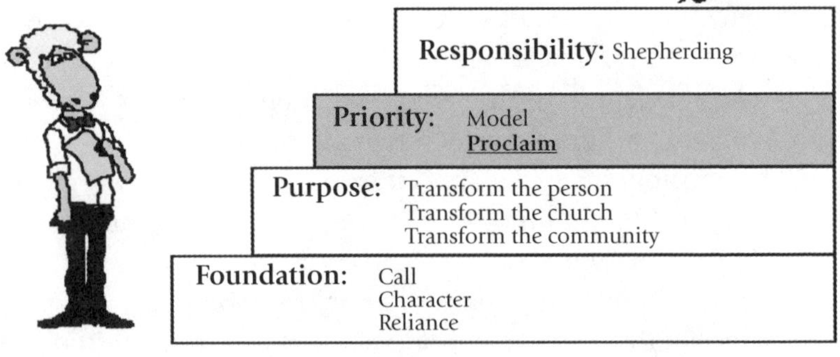

Figure 9.1.

An Effective Leader Is a Preacher of the Word

For the New Testament writers, the proclamation of Scripture is foundational for moral and spiritual transformation. In Paul's exhortation to Timothy, he places preaching at the center of Timothy's activities: "Until I come, devote yourself to the public reading of Scripture, to preaching and to teaching" (1 Tim. 4:13). This exhortation is based on the firm conviction that Timothy would save both himself and his hearers by upholding biblical truth (v. 16). The transformational power of pastoral ministry is, in fact, found in the faithful communication of God's truth. When we preach the Scriptures, we have authority in our message. As Haddon Robinson rightly points out, "Preaching in Paul's mind did not consist of man discussing religion. Instead, God himself spoke through the personality and message of a preacher to confront men and women and bring them to himself. . . . Yet when a preacher fails to preach the Scriptures, he abandons his authority. He confronts his hearers no longer with a word from God but only with another word from men. Therefore, most modern preaching evokes little more than a wide yawn. God is not in it."[3] Preaching is the means by which God delivers the message of redemption. For Paul, preaching was not a discourse of religious ideas, it was the process by which God communicated (Titus 1:3).

When we proclaim Scripture, we minister to people's core needs. In Psalm 119:9–11, the psalmist links righteous living with the application of biblical truth. Preaching is more than a traditional element of the worship service; it is the dynamic means by which God prepares people to avoid and overcome sin. Preaching is an intensely spiritual event. The power to transform is not found in the personality of the leader or the communication skills of the speaker, but in the very nature of Scripture itself. The Bible is not static, needing a communicator to give it life and force. Instead, the Bible is dynamic and powerful. Inherent in its message is the ability to penetrate a person's inner being, changing his or her thoughts and motives (Heb. 4:12). It is not the communicator who gives the message vitality and power; rather, in faithfully explaining and applying God's Word (Isa. 55:11), the communicator unveils the inherent power and vitality of the Bible.

As pastors of small churches, we occasionally question our call to ministry because our preaching is not on a par with that of many well-known preachers who populate the air waves. We typically do not see ourselves as great communicators. As much as we try to sharpen our skills, we will always feel somewhat inadequate in the pulpit. But even if we never master the art of speaking poetically and skillfully, we can still preach powerfully and effectively, because when we faithfully convey God's Word, our message has authority. The power is found in the message itself not in the form in which the message is delivered. This does not deny the importance and value of form and skill, and the need to improve our abilities; but the focus must always remain on Scripture itself rather than on us as communicators. Effective preaching is simpler than we realize; it's a matter of faithful and persistent practice.

An Effective Leader Correctly Handles the Word of God

Preaching is more than just standing up and reading from the Bible. It involves correct understanding and insightful application to people's lives. As Paul admonished Timothy to "preach the Word," he also established the importance of correctly proclaiming God's message: "Do your best to present yourself to God as one approved, a workman who does not need to be ashamed and who correctly handles the word of truth" (2 Tim. 2:15). Effectiveness in ministry involves, therefore, the careful study of Scripture. The apostles recognized the importance of studying and proclaiming the Word when they were confronted with the ever-increasing demands of maintaining the organizational structure of a growing church. They made it clear that the priority of their time as leaders was in the "ministry of the word" (Acts 6:4). The people in our pews may not fully understand and appreciate what is required to preach effectively, and they may not fully understand what constitutes an excellent sermon, but they will "know a bad sermon when they hear it."[4] They know when a sermon is not biblically sound.

Correctly proclaiming the meaning of Scripture involves more than historical and grammatical analysis of the text. In Ezra 7:10, we discover a model for the proper proclamation of Scripture: "Ezra had devoted himself to the study and observance of the Law of the LORD, and to teaching its decrees and laws in Israel." This model points to three principles concerning the role of the communicator:

1. *Study.* Communicating the truth involves study. The term translated "study" comes from a Hebrew word meaning to inquire, investigate, and search out a meaning. This is not merely an intellectual exercise with the goal of mental understanding. The term also carries with it the idea of application and practice. The emphasis is on both understanding and implementation. While genuine study involves both comprehension and application, it is important that the application proceed from the exegesis. Without correct interpretation, the application will be misguided at best, or corrupted, leading people away from a growing relationship with God. To live in a godly way, one must first think biblically.

   As small-church pastors, we tend to be relational by nature. We enjoy small churches because they provide us an opportunity to build relationships with people. We enjoy getting out of the office and visiting people in the community. We need to recognize, however, that our strength in ministry is also a point at which we are vulnerable to misapplied priorities. Although it is important for us to be with people, it cannot come at the expense of the more important responsibility of biblical exegesis. Otherwise, our understanding and proclamation of Scripture can become shallow and faulty. The tension between study and other aspects of ministry is further compounded by the number of times we may be required to prepare messages and Bible studies during the week. As small-church pastors, we do not have the luxury of spending twenty hours a week preparing for each sermon. We may also have to prepare messages for Sunday evening, a midweek service, and a home Bible study. So on the one hand we need to study, and on the other hand we need to be with people—all the while not neglecting our own families.

Although there are no easy answers to this dilemma, and each pastor will need to discover what works best in that pastor's particular setting, some general principles can help. First, we should devote ourselves to spending at least half our time in study and preparation for the various services, with top priority being the Sunday sermons. Second, begin studying the passage at least one to two weeks ahead of time. This will allow time for thinking through the passage. Allowing the passage to sit on the back burner for a while enables us to discover the flow of the passage more easily. Third, focus on exegetical messages rather than topical ones.[5] Preaching and teaching through a particular book of the Bible or a particular passage enables us to keep our messages biblically focused and allows us to address the whole spectrum of human experience. Fourth, we should study a passage long enough to have a clear understanding of its meaning. Robert Thomas cautions, "Many churches are on the rocks because of careless hermeneutics, ignorance of biblical languages, and unsystematic theology. Rough estimates as to what this or that passage means will not do. We need qualified expositors who will take the time and make the necessary sacrifices to do their homework well and bring clarity to the minds of God's people as they read and study God's holy Word."[6] Our task is not to share our ideas but to convey biblically revealed truth.

2. *Practice.* Communicating the truth involves practice. The final test of biblical exegesis is found in the implementation of the principles of the passage in the lives of the speaker and listeners. As Ezra was committed to the "observance of the Law of the Lord," we, before being ready to preach to others, first need to allow the passage to preach to us. As Haddon Robinson points out, "The truth must be applied to the personality and experience of the preacher. This places God's dealing with the preacher at the center of the process. As much

as we might wish it otherwise, the preacher cannot be separated from the message."[7] As preachers, we cannot effectively preach a passage that has not first been applied to our own hearts. If we do not first seek to make the passage relevant to our own lives, our preaching will be shallow and ineffective. As pastors of small churches, our lives are on display for others to see. Both in the church and in the community, people will evaluate our message based upon how much we live it. If they cannot *see* the message first, they will never listen to us, no matter how skillful we are in the pulpit.

3. *Proclaim.* Communicating the truth involves proclaiming the truth to the community. Having understood and applied the law to his own life, Ezra was then ready to "teach its decrees and laws in Israel." Again, the emphasis is on more than public communication. The term *teach* carries with it the idea of training in and getting accustomed to the Law. The task of leadership is to communicate the Bible in such a way that people become trained in living and thinking biblically. This implies more than addressing the mind, but also addressing the will so that people are changed.

An Effective Leader Communicates the Scriptures in All Aspects of Ministry

Communicating biblical truth encompasses the totality of ministry, not just the pulpit. As pastors, we teach biblical truth in five primary ways:

1. *We teach the Word through sermons.* The most significant time for communicating truth is during the weekly sermon. These messages are crucial because they reach the most people. Although at times we may wonder whether our messages are making a difference in people's lives, the testimony of Scripture points to the value of public proclamation (1 Tim. 4:13; 2 Tim. 4:2). The time we spend in preparation for these messages and the delivery of these sermons is not peripheral to our ministry; it is the very core of what we are called to do.

2. *We teach the Word through Bible studies.* As small-church pastors, we can directly minister to those struggling in their faith or those desiring to grow spiritually. A simple Bible study instructing people in the foundational truths of the Christian faith is critical to the success of our ministry. It is the means by which we can help new believers gain a basic understanding of the Christian life. There can also be times of interaction, when we can help people address specific struggles they are having in their lives and in their understanding of Scripture.
3. *We teach the Word through counseling.* Counseling is more than addressing emotional needs through psychological analysis. It is an opportunity for pastors to provide spiritual instruction as we minister to the whole person. If we take seriously Paul's statement that "all Scripture is God-breathed and is useful for teaching, rebuking, correcting and training in righteousness, so that the man of God may be thoroughly equipped for every good work" (2 Tim. 3:16), then we will recognize that Scripture provides the fundamental answers to issues confronting the total person. It does not deal with just the spiritual nature of the individual. Throughout its pages, the Bible provides the foundation for emotional and mental health. Certainly there is value to the study of psychology, a discipline that has contributed much to our understanding of the complexity of the human mind. In our counseling, psychology can supplement but should never replace biblical truth in addressing the total needs of the individual. Separating the emotional and psychological from the spiritual results in a divided personality.

   Because there will always be times when the needs of a particular individual require greater expertise than we as pastors can provide, we should not hesitate to refer people to qualified counselors. We should never think, however, that we have nothing to contribute. Separating the spiritual from the emotional and psychological also results in a divided personality. Even as people receive specialized psychological help, we can provide biblical instruction to address their struggles about God and about the world, and that will be important to their emotional and spiritual healing.

4. *We teach the Word through daily interaction.* As small-church pastors, we interact with people daily. We are not sequestered in sterile offices guarded by secretaries and requiring advance appointments. Instead, we interact informally in places where people are most comfortable. We can ride with them as they take livestock to market. We can have lunch with them at their favorite diner. We can interact around a kitchen table, sharing a cup of coffee and a piece of pie. These are not only times of fellowship; they are occasions when we can share the relevance of God's Word in their daily situations. These informal times are vital for effective leadership because they help people to think biblically in ways that encompass the totality of their lives.
5. *We teach the Word through the example of our lives.* The old cliché, "Actions speak louder than words," speaks volumes of truth. The greatest sermon is not one preached eloquently behind a pulpit, but one lived consistently before others. Our greatest exegesis of the Bible is revealed when we faithfully apply God's truth to our own lives in such a way that people see living examples of how the passage is to be lived and applied. What makes a small church strong is that people in the church and community can examine the pastor's life. They have the opportunity to interact with us during the week, when our words and our actions preach a powerful message.

The call to leadership in the church is a call to marry people's lives to the Word of God. Our ministry will stand or fall on this responsibility.

An Effective Leader Maintains the Centrality of Preaching

Matthew Simpson reminds us of the importance of preaching when he writes concerning preachers, "His throne is the pulpit; he stands in Christ's stead; his message is the word of God; around him are immortal souls; the Savior unseen, is beside him; the Holy Spirit broods over the congregation; angels gaze upon the scene, and heaven and hell await the issue. What associations, and what vast responsibility."[8] The work we do on Sunday and in preparation for Sunday remains the most important and critical element of successful leadership. While character gives validity to our message, our message gives vitality to our ministry.

Preaching is more than just speaking. In involves content (what we say), communication (how we say it), and receptivity (how it is received by the audience). To be effective in preaching, we must have the right subject matter, proclaiming God's will and purpose rather than human philosophy or our own ideas about life. The substance must then be communicated in such a way that the listeners understand God's will and purpose for humanity and God's will for their individual lives. Preaching is the art of taking God's timeless truth and making it relevant to what people will face on Monday morning.

Characteristics of Effective Preaching

Much has been written about the development of sermons to communicate God's truth. Like the most skilled basketball player, who must continually practice the basic fundamentals (such as dribbling and passing), preachers also need to be continually reminded of the fundamentals of effective preaching.

Effective Preaching Is Biblical

In our feel-good, media driven culture, it is easy to preach pop psychology and develop sermons based on what will capture people's attention, that is, what will entertain them or make them feel good. As preachers, we can become more concerned about the medium than the message. Although the medium (how we communicate) is important, it is never more important than the message. When people remember the jokes and stories from a sermon rather than the biblical truth, we have failed in our responsibility. The final test of a sermon is not, Did the people enjoy it? or even, Did they listen? but, Did we communicate God's truth as revealed in the Scripture passage so that people could see its relevance to their lives? A biblical sermon is one in which the message of God, conveyed through the pen of the biblical writer, is faithfully proclaimed by the preacher to address the needs and issues confronting the contemporary audience. The preacher is a bridge between the ancient world and our modern milieu.[9]

Biblical preaching involves both exposition and application. Application without exposition becomes pop psychology, making people feel good about themselves and having positive religious experiences, but never transforming them into the image of Christ. Exposition without application becomes irrelevant, tickling the mind but not addressing the will. Biblical preaching bridges the two. It is grounded in the passage, deriving its form and substances from the text itself; but it is also contemporary in that it applies the timeless biblical message to the present needs and issues of the day.[10]

Effective Preaching Is Theological

Theological preaching involves proclaiming a message that centers on the attributes and actions of God and our required response to him, rather than on man's activities and accomplishments. Although the message is applied to the issues of humanity, the focus remains on God. It is a profound lack that this does not often take place. A study of two hundred evangelical sermons revealed that only 20 percent were grounded in or related to the nature, character, and will of God.[11] The preacher's responsibility is to communicate the theological basis for every principle being taught. Thus, our practice is an outgrowth of our understanding of God. If a principle is not rooted in the character and activity of God, then we need to rethink the principle or reevaluate how it is being communicated. We need to think rightly about God before we can think rightly about ourselves. Only by understanding who God is can we understand who we are, for we are created in his image. Before Paul instructed the church in Ephesus about the importance of congregational unity, the necessity of strong family relationships, and proper attitudes and actions at work (Eph. 4–6), he first established the foundation for such behavior by giving a theological understanding of our new life in Christ (chaps. 1–3). It is only when we understand who we are in Christ that we can begin to understand how we are to live at home, at church, and at work. Paul likewise challenged Timothy to preach doctrinally: "Preach the Word; be prepared in season and out of season; correct, rebuke and encourage—with great patience and careful instruction [i.e., doctrine]" (2 Tim. 4:2).

Effective Preaching Addresses the Will

Preaching is to be transformational, not merely informational. Preaching does not address the mind simply for the purpose of building knowledge. Preaching addresses the mind in order to affect the will for the purpose of transforming character. The mind is the point of engagement because we must think Christianly before we can live Christianly. Preaching is not a mystical experience, bypassing the intellect. On the contrary, truth is rational. As we preach, we communicate to the intellect in order to challenge the will so that a person's character, personality, and behavior might be transformed. In our preaching we are to continually challenge people both to be someone and do something. We are to challenge them to be like Christ and faithfully serve him.

The goal of confronting the will is to lead people into relationship with Christ so they will experience God's redemptive work (1 Tim. 4:16). By addressing the will, we challenge people to answer the question, what must I do in response? As communicators of God's truth we are not impartial, leaving the decision to the listeners. We not only confront them with a decision, but we also exhort them to make that decision, not because of what we think but because of what God demands. Whenever Christ communicated with people, he demanded a response with a decision to be made. The Bible is filled with imperatives that demand a response. Either we do what is required or we rebelliously reject it, but we cannot remain indifferent.

Effective Preaching Challenges People to Change

There can be no growth without change. To remain changeless in the Christian life is to become stagnant. Transformational preaching challenges people to change. When people respond to the message, they should leave the meeting different from when they arrived. When we challenge people with a change of perspective, it should alter their outlook and understanding of God and his activity. Further, they should be challenged to change their perception of other people, so that they respond and behave differently within the church, in the community, and in the world. Moreover, in response to the biblical message, people should change their view of themselves, moving away from their natural, sinful self-centeredness and pride toward humility and a focus on others, which is at the heart of Christlikeness (Phil. 2).

We must challenge people with the necessity of countercultural behavior and action. Although we as believers continue to live in the culture, we are to be distinct in our motives, attitudes, and actions, replacing sinful behavior with righteous living. This involves a change of not only our behavior, but also of our character. Before we experienced God's redemptive work, we were controlled and dominated by sin and our character was marred by the desire for sin. When Christ began his work in us, he began also to imprint his character on us so that we no longer live for ourselves but we live for Christ. God uses transformational preaching as an important ingredient in this process.

Effective Preaching Encompasses the Whole Counsel of God's Word

"All scripture is God-breathed and is useful" (2 Tim. 3:16). As we pastors preach, it is easy to become imbalanced and focus on a single aspect of the Christian life or a particular teaching of Scripture. The Bible, though, is a unified book, not just a collection of significant sayings that have no relationship to one another. Like an excellent cook providing a well-balanced diet, transformational preachers provide their listeners with a well-balanced diet of God's Word. We need to preach from the Old Testament and the New, from the wisdom literature and the historical narratives. At times our sermons will be primarily doctrinal, while at other times they need to address particular issues through topical messages. At times our sermons must focus on confronting sin, but at other times, our sermons proclaim God's unconditional grace and forgiveness. To be effective in the pulpit, we must avoid theological ruts.

Preaching in the Small Church

We don't preach in a sterile homiletical vacuum. We preach in a specific context with a specific congregation who are confronting specific needs. Consequently, our communication methods must be adapted to the setting. When people come into a small church, they come with expectations of the service and the sermon. Effectiveness in a small church setting involves understanding the place of the sermon and the manner in which it is best delivered.

In a Small Church, Preaching Must Be Relational

In a small church, we pastors earn the right to be heard, not by our communication skills, but by our relationships with the people in the congregation. In a larger church setting, people respond to pastors who relate well from the pulpit, who have an ability to connect with the congregation from the platform. In a small church, people respond to pastors who relate well during the week, who have the ability to connect with individuals outside the church building. Although our listeners may enjoy an eloquent preacher, they hear us because we shepherd them during the week.

Our preaching is relational, because the people know us and can relate to us as individuals, and we know them and their needs. As William Willimon and Robert Wilson point out,

> It is axiomatic that the reaction to a sermon is a reaction to the total person. . . . The preacher in the small church can claim and develop this personal base for homiletical authority. In the small church, the people come to know their minister well, often much more than in a large congregation. Consequently, the reaction to the preaching in the small church will be largely a reaction to the pastor as a total person. . . . It is much harder to reject the arguments of someone who is perceived as a close friend, or even as a member of the family, than those of an individual who is

> an outsider. There are few hiding places in the small church. The Word comes with a directness, intimacy, and personality that makes hiding difficult.[12]

It is precisely because we are part of a family and more than just "the preacher" that our message has authority. Preaching is more than a lecture; it is an ongoing conversation between the pastor and the people.

In a Small Church, Preaching Must Be Relevant

People in a small church are not concerned about theoretical truth. They are pragmatists who want to understand how the message of the Scriptures relates to their individual lives. They want relevant truth—relevancy is defined not by what is relevant to society at large, but by what is relevant to the people sitting in the pews. And because we have close, personal relationships with them, we can address specific issues in a way that is loving and compassionate. A sermon is more than an opportunity to communicate biblical truth; it is a time when the pastor can minister to people's needs by applying the Scriptures to their present situations. As preachers, we are the bridge between the text of Scripture and people's lives. We must move beyond generalities, to address specific life situations. Our sermons should thus be delivered in the present tense. People are not interested in what the people in the Bible did; they want to know what they themselves must do. The task of preaching is to show how the actions of people in the Bible and the principles they followed provide answers for our situations today. In order to be effective as preachers, we must expound the biblical text and apply it to the everyday life situations of the people we serve. John Stott warns of two dangers: being biblical without being contemporary, and being contemporary without being biblical. The task of preaching is to be both contemporary and biblical. As Stott summarizes, "We should be praying that God will raise up a new generation of Christian communicators who are determined to bridge the chasm; who struggle to relate God's unchanging Word to our ever-changing world; who refuse to sacrifice truth to relevance or relevance to truth; but who resolve instead in equal measure to be faithful to Scriptures and pertinent to today."[13]

In a Small Church, Preaching Can Be Interactive

One of the benefits of ministering in a small church is that sermons can be interactive. In larger churches, sermons are more like academic lectures in which the speaker communicates truth to a passive audience. But in a small church, the congregation can become active participants in the communication process. This doesn't mean that people will interrupt the sermon (although at times this happens); it means that after the sermon people can interact with the pastor concerning questions they had about the truth that was communicated. Because people in a small church have direct and free access to the pastor during the week, the sermon becomes a dialogue rather than a monologue. When a sermon touches listeners in a specific way, they give us immediate feedback and they interact with us further about their life situations. This enables pastors to take the sermon a step further. The invitation at the end becomes an opportunity to respond to the message and to engage in further dialogue throughout the week.

In a Small Church, Preaching Remains Central to the Service

In a misguided attempt to appeal to feelings, many churches today relegate the sermon to a sideshow of the overall service. The focus has shifted from the proclamation of truth to the experience of the worshipers in song. But because worship involves our responding to God and acknowledging him, hearing the Word is foundational. Although worship certainly includes praising God and rejoicing in his character through song and testimony, the proclamation of truth remains central to everything we as believers do as we gather together. In the early church, they "devoted themselves to the apostles' teaching" (Acts 2:42); the priority of the message was essential. Paul reminded Timothy that the proclamation of God's Word was central to ministry (1 Tim. 4:13). In our small churches, most people come because they want to hear what God has communicated to them, not because they want to be entertained through drama and inspiring music. In our small churches, the worship service still revolves around the message. The rest of the service should either prepare people for the message or provide them with the opportunity to respond to the message.

In a Small Church, Preaching Must Be Simple

People in a small church do not want showmanship or ostentatious language. They want sermons to be readily understood and applied to their lives. This doesn't mean that the sermon should be anti-intellectual, but it should be spoken in a way that people can understand. "Preach to be understood," write Warren Wiersbe and David Wiersbe. "It has well been said that the man who shoots above his target does not prove that he has better ammunition, but only that he cannot shoot."[14] As communicators, we need to use the language of the people, so illustrations should be drawn from what they can relate to. When we refer to theological truths, it should be in terms that are easily understood, rather than technical terms that might impress people with our knowledge but fail to communicate God's message. As communicators, our focus should be on clarity rather than oratory. We may preach impressive sermons, but only clarity and simplicity will result in transformation. Christ was a master communicator in that he spoke profound theological truth in a manner that his listeners could understand and relate to. When describing, for example, the various responses people have to the gospel, he utilized the parable of the sower. When teaching about the penetrating power of the gospel and the subsequent growth of the church, he spoke of yeast and dough.

In our age of church programs built around organizational structure and corporate leadership, we can easily lose sight of our highest priority. Ministry can become so complicated that we lose sight of the simplicity of our task. Ultimately, our task is to imprint God's message in the lives of people. If we fail at this point, we fail in ministry, no matter how grand our vision, how efficient our organization, or how strategic our planning. If we desire to excel in ministry, we must focus on excellence in proclaiming God's message.

When we do not know what else to do in ministry, when we no longer have answers for the perplexities of ministry, we must go back to the fundamental truth proclaimed by Paul: "Preach the Word; be prepared in season and out of season; correct, rebuke and encourage—with great patience and careful instruction. For the time will come when men will not put up with sound doctrine. Instead, to suit their own desires, they will gather around them a great number of teachers to say what their itching ears want to hear. They will turn their ears away from the truth and turn aside to myths" (2 Tim. 4:2–4). Preach the Word. Therein lies the secret to a great ministry.

TEN

The Responsibility of Leadership

Shepherding the Flock

Godly leadership involves more than just preaching good sermons and living godly lives. While preaching and setting a good example are certainly to be a church leader's top priorities, they do not fully define the responsibilities of leadership. In the biblical model, the roles and responsibilities of leadership are compared to those of a shepherd (fig. 10.1). In the shepherding model, the focus is on the well-being of each sheep in the flock (Luke 15:1–7). The model that Christ set for his disciples was focused on spiritual

Building Effective Spiritual Leadership

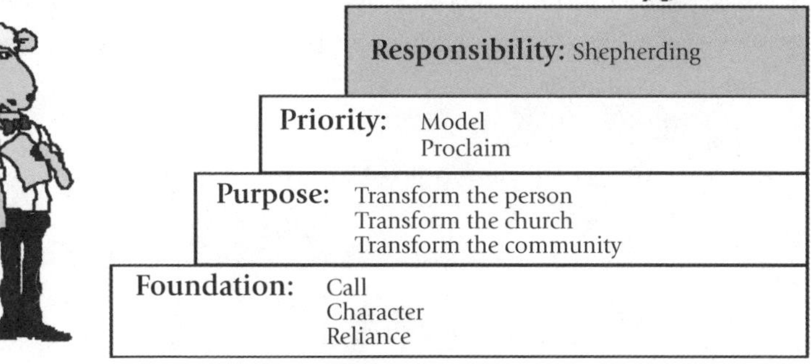

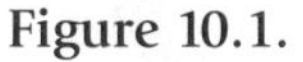
Figure 10.1.

nurture and care, not on strategic planning. Christ did not present seminars on vision casting and organizational management. Instead, he sought to transform the disciples' lives. He corrected their faulty and misguided conceptions about God and about himself. He comforted them in times of turmoil and anxiety. He rebuked their selfish ambitions. He healed their wounds. When they started to stray from God's purposes, he lovingly brought them back.

The Task of Oversight

Throughout the New Testament, the writers place the responsibility of spiritual oversight and care for the well-being of the congregation squarely on the shoulders of the leaders. This responsibility is the same regardless of the size of the congregation, but it is especially important in small churches, where pastors serve without the benefit of additional staff. Although at times this responsibility can be frustrating because we often feel overwhelmed by the task, it is also what makes us so effective in ministering to people's needs. As pastors of small churches, we can provide personal and intentional care, because we have close daily or weekly contact with the people we serve.

Responsible care begins, then, with overseeing the spiritual health of our individual congregations. "Be shepherds of God's flock that is under your care, serving as overseers" (1 Peter 5:2). This task is to be our ongoing objective as we as leaders fulfill our God-ordained duties in the church. Colin Brown points out, "Oversight means loving care and concern, a responsibility willingly shouldered; it must never be used for personal aggrandizement. Its meaning is to be seen in Christ's selfless service which was moved by concern for the salvation of men."[1]

This concept of loving care and concern derives from God's own example. In the Old Testament, God himself watched over and cared for his people (Ruth 1:6; Ps. 80:14–15; Zeph. 2:7). He provided this care not only for the community of his people but also for individuals, such as Sarah in Genesis 21:1. In every instance, the focus of God's leadership is on nurturing and caring, not on administration. This nurturing role was also modeled by Christ, whom Peter refers to as the "Shepherd and Overseer of your souls" (1 Peter 2:25).

The writer of Hebrews states that the church is to "obey your leaders and submit to their authority. They keep watch over you as men who must give an account. Obey them so that their work will be a joy, not a burden, for that would be of no advantage to you" (Heb. 13:17). The reason that we as pastors must give an account is that Christ is the ultimate overseer and he has called us and uses us to accomplish this oversight within the church. When we fail to do our parts, we have not only failed in our roles as leaders in the church, but we have also misrepresented Christ and his watchful care over the church.

Strengthening the Immature and Weak

Oversight begins by strengthening the immature and spiritually weak. When people enter the church, even if they have attended for a number of years, we cannot assume that they have a thorough understanding of God's truth and are applying his truth to their daily lives. If anything, when considering the state of the church today, the opposite must be assumed. It's easy to throw up our hands in frustration and anger because people don't think and live biblically, but we instead must roll up our sleeves and get to work in ministering to them and strengthening them in their faith. In Ezekiel 34:4, God condemns the leaders of Israel for their failure to provide care for the spiritually weak: "You have not strengthened the weak or healed the sick or bound up the injured. You have not brought back the strays or searched for the lost. You have ruled them harshly and brutally." We must provide care for those who have wandered from the truth. When people stop attending our churches, we must do more than bemoan their absence. We must actively pursue them and seek their return—if not to our own congregation, then at least to another that is centered on Scripture (Ezek. 34:5–6; Zech. 11:16).

Comforting the Suffering

In providing care, it is necessary to provide comfort and encouragement to those who are going through stressful events and suffering. Every week, people enter the church doors battered and bruised from their daily spiritual battles. Like a battlefront emergency hospital, the church is a place to treat the wounded and comfort those who have faced trials and struggles.

People enter the church physically affected by the spiritual corruption, devastation, and disease that are all results of the Fall. James writes that someone who is sick is to call upon the elders to "pray over him and anoint him with oil in the name of the Lord" (5:14). James thus establishes the importance of both spiritual and physical care in times of distressing illness. As leaders we are to assist the sick in getting proper medical attention (i.e., anointing the head with oil) as well as ministering to their spiritual needs.[2] When people face serious difficulties, their faith is challenged as they struggle with their understanding of God and how a good God allows bad things to happen to good people. Serious illness is often accompanied by spiritual doubts. Consequently, we as leaders, as part of our spiritual oversight, are to assist people in regaining spiritual perspective.

Directing in Times of Crisis

As leaders, we are to provide direction during times of crisis. Difficulties, conflicts, and struggles are a fact of life and ministry. The sooner we realize this, the better off we will be. At our salvation, we are not placed into a utopian world; we remain in imperfect communities in a corrupt world that suffers the consequences of impure and improper decisions and actions. In our small churches, we face the struggles of declining membership, financial pressures, and ministry discouragement. Our congregations are thrown into upheaval by conflicts, by individuals becoming ensnared in their own corruption, and by the natural human desire for sin. We face personal crises as people challenge and question our authority. The task of leadership is not to abandon people when the going gets tough, but to guide them through the minefields of crisis to the safety of solid spiritual ground.

Shepherding in the Small Church

While the task of providing oversight is universal for all leaders in every church, how we accomplish the task differs greatly in each context. How leaders of small churches provide oversight differs greatly from the same task in a larger congregation. In large churches, leaders provide oversight primarily through program development. They carefully identify the needs in the congregation and then develop programs to meet those needs. In a smaller church, the pastor provides oversight through personal relationships and daily involvement in the lives of each individual in the congregation. The larger the church, the more the leaders will entrust oversight to subordinates and specialized groups. Someone who is struggling with alcohol abuse, for example, receives shepherding care through a specialized ministry for recovering alcoholics. Small churches, on the other hand, do not have such a luxury. Instead, the shepherding ministry must be individual and personal. Consequently, greater emphasis is placed on the pastor's daily and personal interactions with the congregation. In a small church, the leader does not shepherd primarily through formal programs, but through informal interactions. Nevertheless, these activities are neither arbitrary nor haphazard; they require deliberate intent on the part of the leader in four key areas:

1. *Intentional visitation.* To effectively shepherd people in a small church, we must make visitation intentional. "There is a tendency among some recent seminary graduates," writes John Thiessen, "to try to run a church from an office, even a small church. They insist upon having all the most modern equipment in their office and bombard their membership with frequent letters and circulars. This will never take the place of calling. It is still true that 'a house-going pastor will produce a church-going people.'"[3] These words, written more than thirty years ago, are even more true today. Visitation has become the church's lost ministry. E-mails and mass mailings have replaced personal contact. Kennon Callahan, in challenging the church to become more mission oriented by seeing their own community as the mission field, points out that visitation is central to missions. "We need the *new* discovery of visiting with persons in our community. . . . Mission movements share visiting. Institutions hold meetings. The church has never been at its best as an institution. The church has

always been at its best as a mission movement. As we move into the twenty-first century, we are called to take on once more the shape and momentum of the mission movement. Mission movements visit as naturally as people breathe, as regularly as the sun rises and sets."[4]

Perhaps one of the reasons we have lost the art of visitation is because of our perspective of what visitation is. In a pastor's mind, visitation involves going and knocking on a stranger's door, and awkwardly sitting on the couch and talking to someone about that person's need to get right with God. After a time of uneasiness, both the pastor and the person being visited are glad to end the conversation and go their separate ways. Effective visitation is not this type of calling.

Effective visitation is not just a series of formal visits; it encompasses the informal interactions we as pastors have with people as we encounter them in their daily lives and in their environments. It is during these times that we have the opportunity to discuss life and share the reality of Christ in our own lives. Certainly, visitation includes hospital visits, stopping at the home of a shut-in, and going to see a family in crisis (Matt. 25:36; James 1:27), but it is much more than that. It is being available and with people in the daily affairs of life, when we are at school events, when we are hunting together, when we are meeting them for lunch. It is these informal visits that often produce the greatest reward.

But these informal visits do not just happen. We must deliberately set aside time. Otherwise, we can become so busy "doing the work of the church" that we never come in contact with the people of the church. It should not escape our notice that when Christ went to visit Zacchaeus, it was not because Christ had set up a visitation program with his disciples to go door to door; it came because of a natural encounter as Christ was walking down the road.

2. *Intentional follow-up.* To effectively shepherd people in a small church, we must be intentional in our follow-up. It is often said that a small church is hard to get into and hard to get

out of. It is also true that the back door does exist, although it is less traveled in a small church. No matter what size a church is, there will be people who enter the church for a time—sometimes an extended time—and then quietly slip out the back, never to darken the doors again. Typically, their departure is a gradual process, not a sudden occurrence. They don't walk out in a huff one Sunday; instead, they start to miss a Sunday here and there. They become less faithful in their involvement in the church's ministries and activities. Over time, they subtly disassociate themselves from the church so that by the time they actually leave, no one notices.

But that should never happen in a small church. An advantage of being a small-church pastor is that we can maintain a greater pulse on the spiritual struggles people are facing. If we are alert, we can notice the telltale signs that someone is becoming spiritually adrift. But often we are so busy doing the work of ministry that we lose sight of the people we serve. An effective shepherd is one who is intentional, one who takes notice when someone becomes less involved, and one who makes contact with people. Like a shepherd who notices the sheep who have a tendency to wander away and thus keeps a watchful eye on them, so we start to keep closer contact with individuals who might be prone to drift away from the church. Although we cannot stop people from drifting, we will be held accountable for our response (Luke 15:4–7; Jer. 23:2–4; Ezek. 34:4; Zech. 11:17).

3. *Intentional care.* To effectively shepherd people in a small church, we must provide care for those going through personal crises. It may be a farmer who is facing financial ruin because of a drought or a sudden drop in the price of commodities. It may be a family who is dealing with the anxiety of a cancer diagnosis, or a grieving spouse who is faced with the sudden loss of a lifelong mate. It may be a marriage that is struggling because of unresolved conflicts. Crises such as these require a personal visit from the pastor, not just a note. In a larger church, the needs of the congregation often take precedence over the needs of individuals. A senior pastor in a large church cannot

visit every family in crisis. But in a small church, our whole ministry hinges on our willingness to visit people directly. In a small church, individuals are often regarded as more important than the congregation as a whole. A pastor who thinks that being at the midweek prayer service is more important than being at the bedside of a dying parishioner may find that the rest of the congregation questions his concern for them as well. People want to know that we care about them as individuals, not just as a number on the church rolls.

Caring for people in crisis not only involves personal visits and ongoing spiritual care, it may also involve being an advocate for those needing specialized care. In a small church located in an isolated community, there may not be any other social programs to help people in crisis. People have nowhere to turn, and they may not trust an impersonal agency in a neighboring city. Consequently, they will turn to the church for help—and to the pastor in particular—because the pastor is someone who they know cares about them. In order to help people, we may need to become an advocate and voice for them, assisting them in getting the specialized help they need, whether in the area of financial assistance or emotional and psychological care. Caring for people may involve speaking on behalf of a woman who is married to an abusive spouse. It may involve assisting a family whose child has been abused by a neighbor.

4. *Intentional hospitality.* To effectively shepherd people in a small church, we must practice hospitality. Hospitality is more than inviting someone over for a meal; it's opening our homes so that people feel comfortable stopping by any time, frustrating as that may be for us and our families. Hospitality involves availability and accessibility, so that people regard us as more than just their pastor, but also as their personal friend. Although we certainly must at times protect our families from the constant intrusion of ministry, we must also recognize that people want to know us and share with us. If we make our homes our fortresses, protected by a moat of inaccessibility, we will never earn the trust that is essential for spiritual shepherding to occur. In rural areas in par-

ticular, hospitality is not only beneficial, it is expected and necessary. A pastor in a large church earns credibility with the people through his preaching, program development, and the leadership he provides in setting the course for the church. In a small church, the pastor earns credibility for ministry through relationships. If we are aloof, separated from the people by professional detachment and isolation, we will never establish the trust and acceptance necessary for effective ministry.

Hospitality is not something we practice only at home; it is equally important that we model it at church. Because small churches are relationally based, they can be difficult for new people to penetrate. Newcomers sense the strong relational ties and don't always feel welcome. When we ask people involved in a small church to identify the strength of their church, they often reply that it is the friendliness and closeness of the congregation. But when we ask newcomers why they did not go back to that same church, they often reply that the church was not friendly. Congregations do not, of course, desire to exclude newcomers, but when people already have all their relational needs met, they do not actively seek new relationships. Instead of seeking out newcomers to welcome them and enfold them into the congregation, the established members of the church spend all their time with people around whom they are already comfortable. Consequently, it is our task as leaders to be intentionally hospitable with newcomers. We must not only go out of our way to welcome them and invite them into our homes, we must also be the catalyst to introduce newcomers to the rest of the congregation. We can do this by inviting new families for dinner along with other couples from the church who share common interests. Modeling hospitality builds hospitality as the whole congregation begins to see the importance of welcoming new people into the fellowship of the church (Rom. 12:13).

The Task of Administration

Administration has always been the bane of small church pastors. Two characteristics of small churches, which often attract people, are the lack of church politics and the simplicity of the congregational structure. Simplicity, though, can also become shoddy organization. Although small churches can and should remain relational in focus, with simple organizational structures, they must also recognize the importance of proper administration. As David Ray summarizes, "The work of ministry and mission is the *what* and the *why* of the church. The work of church maintenance is the *how, who, when, where,* and *how much does it cost* of church life."[5] The reason why small churches often react negatively to anything smacking of organizational structure is that their pastors have approached organization with a large-church mind-set. If we are to lead and shepherd our small churches effectively, we must recognize that they function differently than larger churches. Douglas Walrath warns, "The widespread belief that those who lead small churches should seek to fulfill visions and apply methods appropriate for large churches is misguided. The differences between the two are profound. To imagine that one will be equipped to lead one kind of church by learning methods that are suitable for another is like imagining that a physician could be prepared to practice psychiatry by completing a residency in urology."[6]

The most significant characteristic of the small church is that it is relationally driven; therefore, pastors must use a different approach in how they organize, structure, and administer the church. Visions, goals, and strategies are critical for every church, even small ones, and much has been written on these issues.[7] Likewise, many organizational basics, such as establishing policies and developing effective structures (e.g., budgets, committees) are necessary, even for a small church. The failure to create some level of organization can, in fact, undermine the effectiveness of the church (1 Cor. 14:40). How we establish organizational goals and direct the operations of the church will determine how effective we will be.

The Importance of a Relational Administrator

The most important dynamic of administration in a small church is that leaders must be relational in their approach rather than organizational or programmatic. Small churches function based on relationships; thus, how we perform our administrative tasks must also be relational. As Douglas Walrath observes, "Their past experience with 'outsiders' makes members of many small churches suspicious of administrators who function 'professionally' and organizationally. Their first concern is not whether an administrator is efficient or effective, but whether he or she is devoted to them. . . . An administrator with minimal skills who belongs in a small congregation will fare far better than one who is highly skilled but detached. Members of small churches will respond with both energy and faith to the devoted ministry of a relational administrator."[8] In short, organizational skills are important but our relational skills are far more important. People in a small church desire a pastor and leader who relates well to them, rather than one who can simply run programs effectively.

Relational Administrators Build on Established Relationships

It's been said that the first year a pastor is in a church provides the greatest window of opportunity for change. This may or may not be true of large churches, but it is certainly not true of small churches. In a small church, the pastor must first learn to appreciate and accept the people and their culture. Only then can he guide the church in the process of making changes, even those deemed most crucial. Many pastors who have worked in small churches would agree that a pastor should be in a church for at least a year before attempting any significant changes. It takes at least a year to learn the culture of the congregation and develop the trust necessary to effectively orchestrate change.

It is wrong to assume that small churches are reluctant to change. Most people are open to change, but not at the expense of relationships. Effective pastors learn to identify and build on established relationships, proposing changes only after properly assessing how the changes will affect these relationships. A certain pianist in the church, for example, may have far greater ability than the current accompanist, whose musical skills are marginal at best. When a new pastor arrives at the church, it may be immediately apparent that the church would be better served by replacing the pianist with someone who is much more gifted and able to play a number of different styles of music. If, however, the pastor attempts to make the switch, he will likely encounter significant resentment and resistance, not only from the current pianist but from the entire congregation. What might seem like a clear and necessary administrative decision encounters opposition from the rest of the church because it upsets a long-established ministry relationship. To remove the pianist from her position would deeply hurt her, which is something the rest of the congregation does not want to happen, even at the expense of the quality of the church's music. A wise leader will first learn how these relationships function before attempting change, so that when a change is made it doesn't come at the expense of prior relationships. In the case of the marginal pianist, the pastor might choose to work with her by teaming her with a more talented musician, or he might help her find a different ministry to which she is more gifted. Or the pastor may leave everything as is, recognizing that, relative to the growth of the church, relational connections will be more beneficial than the quality of music.

To lead effectively in a relational manner, the pastor must also accept the congregation's culture. A thorough understanding of both the church's culture and the culture of the community is a necessary prerequisite for leadership and administration. Developing an outreach program at the county fair, for example, may seem an ideal evangelistic event for the pastor, but he may find resistance because most people in the congregation are already immersed in their own activities at the fair. Planning programs during the calving season will encounter resistance from ranchers, not because they are being unspiritual, but because their livelihood hinges on the survival of the new calves. A lack of cultural understanding and appreciation will eventually lead to an erosion of trust between the pastor and the congregation.

To lead effectively in a relational manner, we must recognize that we develop credibility by how well we relate to people, not by how effective our administration is. A relational administrator recognizes that loving people is far more important for effectiveness than any organizational planning. Many small-church leaders encounter rejection because they have sought to be good administrators without being relational. Consequently, they never build a base of credibility for ministry.

Relational Administrators Enhance Relationships

Relational administrators not only understand and build their administration around relationships; they also seek to enhance existing relationships in the church through their organizational structuring. They recognize that, in a small church, the people take precedence over the organization, and the individual is as important as the whole. In a small church, people are more concerned about the well-being of each individual than they are about the well-being of the organization. As a result, church members will keep a person in a position in the church, even if the person is incompetent for that position. Instead of making a change, the members will quietly buttress the person's incompetencies by doing much of the work themselves. This can lead to considerable frustration for us as pastors as we seek to move the church forward in effective ministry.

We must remember, however, that a small church defines effectiveness by how well relationships in the church are developing, not by how smoothly the organization runs. People are attracted to a small church, after all, because of its close relational ties, not by the number and effectiveness of the programs. To sacrifice relationships for the sake of "effectiveness" would undermine the very strength of the small church. Consequently, as we pastors organize and operate our small churches, we must be intentional and purposeful in building relationships even as we organize. In planning a leadership retreat, for example, we should focus as much on building strong relationships as on evaluating the structure of the church. This does not mean that we neglect evaluating the church, but we realize that all the leaders in the church will be more effective in evaluating and leading the congregation if they have close relational connections with each other. Going out for pizza and bowling may be more effective in strengthening the leadership and organizational structures of the church than spending an evening drafting a vision statement and setting goals for the coming year. The stronger the relational bonds among the leadership and in the congregation, the more effective everyone will be in developing and accomplishing a vision and goals for the overall ministry of the church.

Relational Administrators Focus on Function Rather Than Form

Small churches are practical rather than theoretical. They are more concerned about what works than about how it works or why it works. They are more concerned about function than about form. Small churches are more concerned with effectiveness than efficiency. When examining proposed changes, people often will say, "But we've always done it that way." They resist, not so much because they are bound to past traditions but if something worked well enough in the past, why change it? They live by the adage "If it ain't broke, don't fix it." It's important to realize, though, that this statement is vastly different from "If it's running efficiently, don't fix it." By "ain't broke," they don't necessarily mean that everything is running efficiently; it just means that things are going well enough. For many rural churches, the question is not, Can we do this more effectively? but, Is this accomplishing what we want? Before we as pastors can effectively restructure and reorganize a small church, we must be able to demonstrate to the people that the ministry needs restructuring not just to be more efficient but because it is not accomplishing what the church desires.

The Importance of a Simple Organization

People are attracted to a small church because it is not a complex organization. They enjoy a small church because of its back-to-basics simplicity. The challenge for small-church leaders is how to maintain a simple organization while dealing effectively with organizational issues. People in small churches tend to resist formalized policies and procedures, even when those policies and procedures are necessary. Many small churches are reluctant, for example, to develop a child abuse policy for their Christian education programs, even when it's necessary for legal protection. Likewise, auditing the church's books is seen as mistrusting the treasurer's integrity, even though it protects the treasurer from false accusations. Written contracts are often viewed as unnecessary, because "a man's word is sufficient." Effective leadership nevertheless requires that a church have organizational structure and sound business practices. In an age in which the church is increasingly scrutinized, a failure to have sound financial standards can even in rural areas undermine the church's credibility in the eyes of the community. Therefore, it is important for church leaders to develop policies and procedures.

In establishing credible structures and policies in a small church, it is important, though, not to overorganize. Several principles should be kept in mind.

1. Recognize that some policies are necessary for the protection of the church. Failure to have a policy on child abuse not only opens the church for potential lawsuits that can destroy the church financially, but it also undermines the credibility and witness of the church in the community.
2. Keep policies and organizational structures to a minimum. Carefully deal with the issues that are mandated, but don't overanalyze. The church can still function effectively with handshakes and oral agreements. Having formal job descriptions may be efficient, but they may be viewed as controlling. In many cases, it is better to have informal policies that are not written down per se but are verbalized in an informal setting. These policies are not hard-and-fast rules, but guidelines that may be changed depending on the situation. Having informal policies governing the budget may be beneficial, but in a small church, the budget is typically a suggested guideline. What really determines how money is allocated is the need of the moment rather than the budget.
3. Keep the organizational structure flexible and simple. Having five committees to oversee various ministries does not make sense when there are only twenty-five people in the church. One or two committees may be all that is needed. Additional committees can be formed as the church grows and it becomes necessary.

The Task of Equipping

The church was never meant to be like a cruise ship, where a few do the work for the pleasure and ease of the rest. It is more like a fishing boat where everyone has a task and responsibility to perform. The task of leadership is not to do all the work so that the rest of the body can rest in ease; it is to equip the congregation so that everyone is appropriately involved. Concerning leadership, Paul writes that we are "to prepare God's people for works of service, so that the body of Christ may be built up" (Eph. 4:12). This directive defines the purpose of leadership and the desired result. The purpose (Greek: *pros*) of leadership is to prepare people for the end result (Greek: *eis*)—performing works of service that build up the body of Christ. The word *prepare* connotes mending and repairing in order to make fit for service.[9] Thus, our task is not to look for people who are competent for service; it is to work with individuals who are incompetent in order that they might become competent. One of the strengths of the small church has always been the high degree of congregational involvement. In a small church, no one is—or is allowed to be—a sideline player. Everyone is involved. That involvement, however, often is not accompanied by sufficient preparation. As long as people are willing to serve, we pastors give them responsibility without necessarily equipping them for the task.

Equipping People Spiritually

Discipleship is not a program; for pastors, it is a process of imprinting our lives on the lives of others. This can only be accomplished effectively to the degree that Christ has imprinted his life on ours (1 Cor. 11:1). In a small church, discipleship happens through the relationships we build in the church. Without positive, intimate relationships, we will never establish credibility with the people. Without credibility and trust, they will never allow us to change their lives through our preaching, teaching, and daily interaction. They will remain polite and even appreciative, but our preaching and teaching will have little real effect on them.

If they listen, it will not be because we stand in front of them on Sunday morning with the title of Pastor; it will be because they know our character and therefore trust our teaching. They will listen because they have seen that we not only practice what we teach, but we also love them and are concerned about their best interests. They will listen because they know we are not seeking to manipulate them to satisfy our own agendas but are leading them to attain God's best for them. This degree of trust and confidence does not come from a position or a program, but from the bond of friendship and trust we have established.

This is not to say that programs and discipleship materials have no place in a small church. They do. Many of the materials available today are excellent and should be used in our discipleship efforts. But these programs will only have value and be effective if we pastors have in-depth connections with people. Nevertheless, in using these discipleship programs in small churches, especially in rural areas, we must keep in mind several important principles:

1. A program that incorporates several short-term commitments is better than a program that extends over a lengthy period of time. People are typically reluctant to commit themselves to a thirty-five-week program. This is especially true in rural areas where farm and ranch schedules provide limited windows of free time for meeting together. In farming communities, spring work begins in early April and lasts until late October. Days are filled with long hours, and six-day workweeks are common. When a month-long calving season and special holidays are thrown in, scheduling a weekly meeting time is almost impossible. It is better to agree on a four- or six-week commitment for discipleship, rather than a thirty-five-week program that will be constantly interrupted.
2. A discipleship program must be practical and hands-on, rather than theoretical and academic. Many people in rural areas work with their hands and deplore spending time in an office. Although they are often highly educated and spend a great deal of time studying market trends, they may not be avid readers. Discipleship programs that involve a great deal of reading may be difficult to implement. For them, information is

not gleaned through a book, but over a cup of coffee, discussing the practical realities of Christian living. They are motivated to learn when they see a program's relevance to life. Theology is important and needs to be taught, but if it is not practical it will be viewed as unimportant.

3. Discipleship must be both formal and informal, with the informal being the primary means. Formal discipleship (i.e., meeting weekly and going through a discipleship manual) is beneficial. Nevertheless, the primary means of discipleship will be informal. Sitting at a diner may afford more opportunities for practical discipleship than meeting weekly at the church. When, for example, a farmer is facing sprouted wheat and declining prices that threaten the future of the family farm, an informal conversation over a cup of coffee might be more conducive for teaching about the sovereignty and providence of God in a way that is both practical and relevant.

Equipping People for Practical Ministry

The challenge facing many pastors today is the challenge of training people for ministry. Many small churches do not have trained people in key positions of leadership. At times, people are appointed to leadership because that role has traditionally been held by others in their families, not because they themselves are gifted and trained. A man might be appointed to a position on the board, for example, because his father served faithfully in that capacity for many years. In another case, a song leader might be selected not because he knows music and sings well, but because "maybe if he is given the role, he will be more faithful in coming to church." A Sunday school teacher might be ill-equipped to teach children, but there is no one else to do the work. In large churches, specialists who do one thing well are valued, and the emphasis is on quality and excellence. In a small church, generalists are valued, and they are called upon to perform a number of different roles, even if their skills are average at best. Our task as pastors of small churches is not to remove the generalists from their positions, which would only alienate us from the congregation and undermine our credibility, but to equip and train them for ministry.

Because small churches run relationally, it often is difficult for new people, lacking the relational connections, to penetrate the ministry hierarchy. The task of leadership, then, is to develop an atmosphere in which people are accepted and assimilated into the ministry of the church.

Another problem in assimilating people into small-church ministry is that even established members often see the work of the ministry as the pastor's responsibility, whereas their own jobs are to work on the farm. Although they have ownership in the church in that they desire to see the ministry succeed, they see the pastor as responsible for its success. Assimilating people into ministry begins when we as pastors teach people about the importance of everyone's involvement in ministry. The work of the church is a team effort, not an individual sport, and it requires everyone's involvement (1 Cor. 12:18). Once people are involved in ministry, we must work to develop their effectiveness. This means working with them, often informally, to train and equip them for ministry. It means offering counsel and advice as they encounter problems and difficulties, and connecting them with others who may have solutions to their problems.

Equipping the church for ministry must include training the board for ministry. Often, the board members in a small church function more as facility managers than spiritual leaders. More time is spent in discussing the upkeep of the church property than in addressing the spiritual needs of the people or in prayerfully seeking God's direction on how to meet those needs. Consequently, we have the task of training the board to be spiritual leaders in the church, teaching them to think biblically and theologically. Board members must be challenged and encouraged to become students of theology, because it is their responsibility to uphold the theological integrity of the church. They must also be trained in the area of ministry involvement. Board members must learn how to evaluate the health of the church and to be involved in strengthening the church. This often can be done on a weekend retreat or by taking fifteen minutes of each board meeting to conduct training on a particular area of ministry.

Equipping People Organizationally

Equipping people for ministry requires that the church provide them with organizational support and the resources necessary to perform the ministry. This begins with spiritual support through prayer. The task of leadership and the church as a whole is to pray for the people who are involved in the various ministries of the church. Prayer is the most important support we can give to people in ministry. It is a profound failing that in many churches prayer has been relegated to a secondary role. The challenge we face in meeting the spiritual needs of our congregations is to develop board members who pray for the ministry of the church as well as for the spiritual, emotional, and physical needs of the congregation. We must make prayer central to all our board meetings, in order to reinforce that prayer is the board's most important task.

Equipping people organizationally involves providing the financial resources to perform the ministry. Here remains one of the constant struggles of the small church. Because small churches operate with very limited resources, it is paramount that the church think realistically about the scope and number of its ministries. Because of the unspoken pressure to be all things to all people and become mini-megachurches, small churches often try to duplicate the multiplicity of programs offered in larger churches. But it's far better to do a few things well than to attempt so much that it stretches to a breaking point the congregation's resources of people, finances, and time. The key is to do one or two things that will have the greatest impact, to do them well, and to make sure the resources are available to do them. In providing the necessary resources, small churches need to think creatively about obtaining the resources. Borrowing a video series for couples from a larger church, for example, will enable a smaller church to have a program with little cost. Creatively adapting old Sunday school material can enable a small church to have a vacation Bible school program without the expense of purchasing an expensive program. When seeking to provide resources, ministry leaders must keep in mind that God will always provide the resources necessary to accomplish what he intends.

The responsibilities of administration, oversight, and training must be done in the context of spiritual care. The purpose is not to build an efficient organization or ministry, but to provide spiritual oversight and care for the congregation so that the congregation is becoming more mature and Christlike in its attitudes, actions, and ministry.

Figure 10.2. Shepherding Responsibilities

ELEVEN

The Context of Leadership

The Small Church

There remains a vast difference today between what is written about leadership and the type of leadership accepted by small-church congregations. Many churches have adopted a managerial model of leadership that focuses on decision making, administration, and vision casting. Although much can and should be learned from the managerial paradigm of leadership, this model often conflicts with the concepts of leadership that prevail in small churches. Consequently, small churches are often perceived as old fashioned, hardheaded, unchangeable, and unleadable—or worse, downright sinful. The problem, however, is not so much with the people as it is with the failure of church leaders to understand the different pattern by which small churches operate.

Spiritual leadership is not conducted in a sterile vacuum in which every situation has the same context. Instead, how we as leaders lead will be greatly influenced by the cultural setting of our churches and the expectations of the people in those churches. Effective leaders understand their specific setting, discern the dynamics of the culture, and fulfill the biblical mandate within that context. Effective spiritual leaders build a bridge between their contemporary settings and the biblical mandates of leadership, effectively leading from within the cultural context without compromising biblical principles. As we view leadership through the biblical lens and our cultural lens, we must seek to keep the biblical lens free from distortion and independent of the cultural lens, while at the same time recognizing the presence and validity of the cultural lens (cf. fig. 1.1). Paul understood this, stating that he had become all things to all men so that by all possible means he might save some (1 Cor. 9:19–23). Effective leadership is not accomplished in the absence of culture but in the context of culture.

Understanding the Small Church Paradigm

Whereas much of what is written about church leadership follows a managerial model, small churches operate under a family model of leadership in which relationships form the fabric of the community and organization. Just as leadership is vastly different in a family owned and operated business compared to a Fortune 500 corporation, the roles and responsibilities of leaders in a small church are perceived much differently than in a megachurch. This is not to say that one is better than the other, but each is appropriate in its own context, and leaders in both situations can learn much from each other. If pastors and board members want to be effective leaders, however, they must understand the criteria by which their congregation judges and views their leadership. Failure to do so will result in unnecessary misunderstandings, bringing frustration and hurt to the pastor, the board, and the congregation.

In the Managerial Model, Management Is by Objectives; in the Family Model, Management Is by Relationships

Management by objectives means that leaders formulate goals and objectives that become the basis for decisions. Plans are made based on desired outcomes. Any decision that does not result in achieving the objectives is rejected. Only those decisions that move the group closer to the accomplishment of their goals are validated. Within a small church, decisions are not based on corporate objectives, but on the effect the decisions will have on the unity and fellowship of the congregation. No matter how significant or beneficial a decision might be, it will be rejected if it is perceived to undermine or threaten the unity within the community. So, for example, a decision to replace the organ with a keyboard would not be based on the objective of reaching baby boomers, but on how it would affect the family who donated the organ and the person who has been playing the organ for the past twenty years.

Within a managerial paradigm, the leaders are the visionaries and direction setters. In the family model, the congregation sets the vision and the leaders serve as facilitators and guides who assist the congregation in determining and implementing its vision.

Most of the literature today dealing with the vision and direction of the church reflects a model adapted from the business community. Pastors are seen as responsible for setting the direction and vision for the congregation, and the congregation then follows the pastor and assists in implementing the vision. George Barna, quoting Bill Moore, writes, "The leader's got to have a vision of where he plans to take the company. He has to be able to dramatize that vision for his organization."[1] In Barna's model, pastors function like company leaders in determining the direction for the church. As the pastor communicates the vision to the board and congregation, they rally around him in moving the church forward.

By contrast, small churches often balk at a pastor who attempts to dictate a direction for the congregation. In the family model of leadership, direction is based on input from the entire group, with each family member having a say in the matter. The role of the pastor, in this model, is not to set the direction, but to help the congregation establish its own direction and to make sure that the direction reflects biblical reality. In this model, the people, not the pastor, set the vision for the congregation. The pastor is responsible to work with various subsets of the congregation to implement that vision. Small churches typically want a pastor who listens to their visions and dreams and works with them in achieving their objectives.

In the Managerial Model, the Pastor Serves as the CEO; in the Family Model, the Pastor Serves as a Shepherd

Small churches want pastors who will relate to the congregation as individuals. They look for someone who will minister to them personally rather than through programs. They want a leader who is approachable and who provides guidance and comfort through the struggles and pressures of daily life. While the pastor may oversee various programs and ministries, the people are more concerned about his relational skills than about his managerial skills. In the managerial model, a pastor's performance is evaluated based on his effectiveness in supervising programs and setting the direction for the church's ministries. In the managerial model, it is more important for a pastor to minister to the entire congregation than to each individual. In a small church, how the pastor ministers to each individual in the congregation is more important than how he ministers to the whole congregation. People in a small church evaluate how much time the pastor spends with them. They want to know the pastor personally and individually. They are not content to leave messages with his secretary or be referred to another staff member. They want the pastor accessible and available.

In the Managerial Model, Organizational Plans Dictate Policies and Procedures; in the Family Model, Relationships Dictate Policies and Procedures

The managerial model operates on the assumption that the organization's health and well-being is more important than those of the individual. Procedures are determined by the effect they will have on the whole organization. Consequently, policies and procedures are designed to protect the organization and keep it running smoothly. In a small church, based on a family model of leadership, the assumption is that individuals are more important than the whole organization. It is not that the importance of the organization is not recognized, but the health and well-being of the individual is seen as having a significant effect on the health and well-being of the whole group. If one person is dissatisfied or upset, the whole congregation experiences tension and the group dynamics are drastically altered. Consequently, policies and procedures are established to assure the health of individual members and to protect them from harm, even at the expense of organizational effectiveness.

In the Managerial Model, Success Is Measured by Programs and Growth; in the Family Model, the Focus Is on Stability and Unity

Churches that operate under a managerial model measure success by results. They are product oriented rather than process oriented. The managerial church is considered evangelistic if baptisms are occurring. Growth and success are measured by the number of programs developed and the number of people participating in these ministries. Thus, people evaluate the health of the congregation by its location and visibility, the percentage of people involved in small groups, the stability of the financial resources, the adequacy of the facilities, and the development of multifaceted programs. If numbers are increasing, people are satisfied because the church is growing. When numbers decrease, the people become dissatisfied because the church is perceived as declining.

In the family model, success is measured by relationships and inward experiences. The congregation is process oriented rather than product oriented. The congregation is considered to be evangelistic if people are sharing Christ with their neighbors and are involved in the community, even if that activity does not translate into baptisms and the addition of new members. The church is considered successful when there is unity in the congregation and when people are caring for one another. Health is measured by the absence of conflict, the stability of the membership rolls, the willingness of people to be involved, and the amount of personal growth they experience. Regardless of the numbers, people are satisfied as long as each individual is growing.

In the Managerial Model, a Few People Make Most of the Decisions; in the Family Model, the Congregation Makes Most of the Decisions

The larger the church, the more decisions are made by delegation. The congregation is responsible to elect people to serve on the various boards, but the boards are responsible for most of the decisions. The people decide only the most significant issues that affect the entire congregation and the future of the church. In a small church, everyone is considered to have an equal voice, and the congregation makes most of the decisions. Boards and committees make only minor decisions and then only after the congregation has carefully delineated the scope of those decisions. Boards are responsible for researching issues and bringing recommendations to the congregation, but it is the congregation that has the final say. In the managerial model, as applied in the church, decisions are made by the whole only when they affect the whole. In the family model, decisions are made by the whole even when they affect only a part.

In the Managerial Model, the Budget Guides Decisions; in the Family Model, Decisions Guide the Budget

When a business contemplates a proposal, one of the first considerations is how the idea will fit within the budget. Although finances are not the sole determining factor, they do weigh heavily in the process. The formation of a new budget for the coming year is an important process and is given careful consideration. In the family model, the budget plays a far less significant role. In many small churches, budgets are made but rarely followed. People give based on needs rather than on the budget. The budget serves only as a general guideline. When needs arise and proposals are made, decisions are based on the present financial status rather than on a future budget. When there is a need, the congregation readily alters the budget rather than restricting it based on future budgeted needs.

In the Managerial Model, Groups Function Independently; in the Family Model, Groups Function Interdependently

In the managerial model, the whole comprises a number of different groups that function independently of each other. Only when their function and purpose affects the entire congregation, or another group, is there mutual discussion and interrelatedness. In the family model, each group is an interrelated part of the whole. As a result, every decision of one group is of interest to the other groups, even when that decision does not have any direct bearing on those other groups. People in the Christian education department desire to know what the worship group is doing, because they see their work as part of worship and want to coordinate efforts.

Leading in the Family Model of Leadership

Small churches function, then, as families rather than as businesses. For pastors and other church leaders who desire to work effectively within this model, there are exhilarating rewards and exasperating frustrations. The depth of enjoyment that comes from the close bonds between members in a small church is priceless. But for pastors and leaders who strive to move the church forward in the accomplishment of the Great Commission, the family model at times smacks of dogged exclusiveness and unbending traditionalism. Can a small church function under the family model of leadership and still be effective in ministry? Surprisingly, some people would say no. For them, the only proper course of action is to change the model and transition the church to be more progressive and task-oriented. More often than not, this approach results in congregations and pastors becoming frustrated and hurt, as both perceive the other as hardheaded and demanding.

Accepting the family model of leadership and learning to understand and serve within that model are essential to leadership in a small church. The task of leadership is not to force people to follow, but to create an atmosphere where they desire and are willing to be led, where they trust the leadership and are willing to support the leadership. This can only come through understanding what the people expect of their leaders and serving within the context of those expectations.

Qualities of a Family Model Leader

For us to be effective as family model leaders, certain qualities must govern our activities and our approach to the church. Just as the pastor of a large congregation must demonstrate certain skills and abilities to be effective in overseeing a large organization, so too the pastor of a small church must demonstrate certain skills and abilities that are necessary for effectiveness in the small-church context.

Family Leaders Lead by Example

Small church leaders have personal contact with everyone in the congregation. Because of this interaction, the daily lives of the pastor and other leaders are open for constant inspection and evaluation. As earlier noted, leaders earn the right to lead when they establish a pattern to follow. The apostle Paul understood the importance of leadership by example, writing on numerous occasions for people to follow his example as he followed Christ (1 Cor. 11:1; Phil. 3:17; 2 Thess. 3:7). Likewise, when writing to young pastors, he challenged them to be worthy models for their congregations to follow (1 Tim. 4:12; Titus 2:7). Setting an example encompasses two critical areas. First, the leader must be a mature disciple of Christ, one who submits all aspects of life to the authority and guidance of Scripture. Second, the leader must exemplify the type of commitment and dedication—in both time and energy—needed if the church is to accomplish its mission.

Family Leaders Lead Through Servanthood

While Paul gives the responsibility of leadership in the home to husbands, he makes it clear that genuine leadership is not dictatorial but sacrificial (Eph. 5:22–33). Servant leaders are not concerned about their own success; instead they sacrifice themselves completely for the success of others, as Christ did for the church (Eph. 5:25). A servant leader is one who is not concerned about the accomplishment of his or her own agenda, but is dedicated to assisting people in the achievement of their dreams and plans. Servant leaders strive to assist people, fitting themselves into the schedules of others rather than fitting others into their schedules. Servant leaders do not write people off when they fail to measure up to expectations; instead, they come alongside people and help them grow into the job. They do not take offense when people express frustrations; instead, they listen carefully and find ways to help.

Family Leaders Learn to Be Relational

The writer of Proverbs wisely points out that the security and stability of the king is found in his willingness to love people: "Love and faithfulness keep a king safe; through love his throne is made secure" (20:28). To be effective, small-church leaders must learn to be relational, grounding their leadership on the development of strong personal relationships with the people whom they serve. Relational leadership encompasses five critical characteristics:

1. *Relational leaders love deeply.* Being motivated by love involves having a deep love for Christ, a love that springs forth from his love for us (2 Cor. 5:14). When we love Christ, we learn to love his bride, the church. What motivated Paul to write an undoubtedly difficult letter to the Corinthians, one that taxed him emotionally and threatened his relationship with the church, was the deep love he had for them (2 Cor. 2:4). Love for the church is built on our love for individuals. It is not enough to say we love the church; we must love the people who make up the church, including those who are problematic and difficult to love. Some people are abrasive, some are unloving, some are obnoxious, but the call to leadership is a call to love them all.
2. *Relational leaders accept people.* Acceptance does not mean we give blanket approval to everything people might do. That would be unloving and selfish. Yet, before we can guide people through the process of change, we must accept them for who they are. This involves learning to understand and value their particular subculture. A pastor who moves into a farm community without learning the pressures that farmers face and the way they view life will have a short tenure as a leader. Being accepting is central to receiving trust, and without trust a leader will never be able to effectively guide a congregation.
3. *Relational leaders must be good listeners.* Although biblical leaders are called to be communicators of truth, listening comes before speaking. In the book of Proverbs, a person who presumes to speak before he or she has listened is regarded as a fool. Thus the sage writes, "He who answers before listening—that is his folly and his shame" (Prov. 18:13). Effective lead-

ers learn the story of a church before they attempt to radically change it.

4. *Relational leaders are personal.* They are not afraid to allow people to get close to them. They do not hide behind the office door. Relational leaders are willing to spend time with people, willing to visit them, and willing to invite them into their homes. They are approachable and do not show irritation when interrupted. They are not afraid to be vulnerable by sharing their struggles.
5. *Relational leaders value each individual as much as they do the whole congregation.* In Scripture we see a constant interplay between the community of God's people and the individual's personal relationship with God. While God is the shepherd of Israel (Ps. 28:9) he is also "my" shepherd (Ps. 23:1). Both the community and the individual are equally important to God and are given equal attention. Relational leaders learn to value the contribution and worth of each person, and not place the community above the individual. Neither do they emphasize the value of the individual at the cost of the community. At times leaders must, of course, focus primarily on the community, and other times they must spend time with specific individuals. Throughout, they never neglect one or the other.

Family Leaders Are Patient

"Preach the Word; be prepared in season and out of season; correct, rebuke and encourage—with great patience and careful instruction" (2 Tim. 4:2). Family leaders do not force people to change; they carefully assist people in changing. They patiently wait until people are ready. They work within an individual's capacity to process information and accept change, rather than imposing their own expectations.

Family Leaders Are Teachers

Effective leaders do not assume that people will accept their ideas and changes merely because the leader made suggestions. Instead, leaders recognize that before growth can occur, there must be careful instruction (2 Tim. 4:2). Often the failure of people to accept change is not a result of their unwillingness to change. Rather, it results from the leaders' failure to adequately teach the people why the change is necessary, how to implement those changes, and how to maintain the newly developed plans and strategies.

Leading and Decision Making in the Family Model

Just as a small church approaches leadership differently than a large church, so also the process by which decisions are made reflect a family—rather than a managerial—orientation. Just as a father makes decisions differently at home than he would in the business world, a small church makes decisions differently than would a church governed according to a managerial model. To be effective shepherds, we must understand those differences.

Family Leaders Encourage Participative Leadership

Although a family has a designated leader, decisions that affect the whole family require everyone's participation in the decision making process. A husband does not decide to move across the country without input from his wife and children. Participation means that everyone interested in the decision or affected by the decision is given the opportunity to share his or her ideas and concerns before plans are formulated.

Family Leaders Gain Acceptance for Decisions Before Implementing Them

Making decisions strictly by a majority vote can easily alienate family members. When moving across the country, the husband, wife, and two small children may be in favor of the move, but the teenaged daughter may find the idea of changing schools unacceptable and threatening. To move without her acceptance will only invite rebellion and further conflict in the home. It would be far better to gain her acceptance before the move is made. Although she may not be in favor of the move, she may accept the transition, thus supporting the decision in the long run. The family leader recognizes that a majority vote may get the issue passed, but it requires acceptance by the whole congregation before it will be fully embraced and implemented.

Family Leaders Work with the "Tribal Chiefs"

In most small congregations, certain individuals exert great influence over the rest of the community by virtue of their positions or their family relationships. These individuals may or may not hold an official office, but everyone else will nevertheless look to them for guidance. In most cases, the tribal chief will not be the pastor; it will be someone who has a long history in the church. Effective leaders learn to accept the position and influence of these individuals, and are not threatened by them, but learn to work with them and through them.

Family Leaders Recognize the Value of Informal and Personal Communication

The most important time of family communication is when everyone is sitting around the dinner table sharing the events of the day. The best time for parents to interact with their teenagers is created not by sitting down and saying, "Let's talk." Usually, that's the best way to get a teenager to clam up. Instead, the most significant interactions come when a father and son are working on the car together, or a mother and daughter are working on a project together. The same is true in a small church. Notes in the bulletin, announcements from the pulpit, and letters sent to the congregation are all helpful means of communication, but the most important and effective communication occurs over a cup of coffee through face-to-face interaction. Effective leaders recognize that they need to spend time with people, sharing plans and goals long before attempting to implement them.

Family Leaders Keep the Organization Subservient to Relationships

A father's decision to take a new job is not determined by the economic gains the advancement will bring, but by the positive and negative effects the new job will have on the family. The same is true in a family church. The ultimate question is not, What is best for the organizational church? but, What is best for the individual relationships in the church? Replacing the organist with a worship team may be the right thing to do organizationally, but it might damage relationships, undercutting the vitality and strength of the small church.

Conclusion

With all that has been written on leadership today, pastors have nonetheless lost sight of the simplicity of ministry. The task of spiritual leadership may not be easy, but neither is it complicated. When God called us to serve as leaders in the church, he did not give us the responsibility to build the church. Instead, he gave us the responsibility to proclaim his Word in order that people might be transformed into the character of Christ. This proclamation comes in both our spoken word, as we preach the Scriptures, and through our lives, as we live our faith visibly before others. When we do faithfully proclaim and model the truth of God's Word, our ministry will be successful regardless of the outward results or the size of the church we serve. Although we should seek to maximize our abilities through training and personal growth, we must also recognize that ultimately we can do nothing of our own accord; it is God's working through us that brings to fruition the work of our ministry.

We do not need to know all the answers. When we experience difficulties in ministry, when we face problems that leave us unsure of what to do, we must remember our most important priority in ministry, the hinge on which our ministries swing—the faithful proclamation of Scripture. When we point people to Scripture so that their lives are being changed to conform to the image of Christ, then we will be "good minister[s] of Christ Jesus, brought up in the truths of the faith and of the good teaching that you have followed" (1 Tim. 4:6). Ministry is really simple; it's a matter of preaching the Word, loving the people, and living our lives as examples for others to follow.

Notes

Chapter 1: Returning to an Old Paradigm

1. David Wells, *No Place for Truth* (Grand Rapids: Eerdmans, 1993), 233.
2. W. Bingham Hunter, "What Works? Versus What Does the Bible Say," unpublished article, Western Seminary faculty retreat, Portland, Ore., August 26, 2003.
3. John Piper, *Brothers, We Are Not Professionals* (Nashville: Broadman and Holman, 2002), xii.
4. Glenn Wagner, *Escape from Church, Inc.* (Grand Rapids: Zondervan, 1999), 24.
5. Wells, *No Place for Truth,* 228.
6. Piper, *Brothers, We Are Not Professionals,* 3.
7. Steve Bierly, *How to Thrive as a Small Church Pastor* (Grand Rapids: Zondervan, 1998), 59.
8. Eugene Peterson, *Working the Angles: The Shape of Pastoral Integrity* (Grand Rapids: Eerdmans, 1987), 2.
9. C. E. B. Cranfield, *Romans,* International Critical Commentary (Edinburgh: T. and T. Clark, 1986), 626. Although some might debate such a narrow view of the term as used in this context, and it may involve a broader scope of meaning, care must be taken not to incorporate modern definitions of leadership into the biblical text. Instead, Scripture must be allowed to define spiritual leadership for us.
10. Robert Saucy, *The Church in God's Program* (Chicago: Moody, 1972), 118.
11. Wagner, *Escape from Church, Inc.,* 47.
12. Ibid., 42.

Chapter 2: Ministry

1. Steve Bierly, *How to Thrive as a Small Church Pastor* (Grand Rapids: Zondervan, 1998), 103.
2. Eugene Peterson and Marva Dawn, *The Unnecessary Pastor* (Grand Rapids: Eerdmans, 2000), 60–61.
3. Eugene Peterson, *Working the Angles: The Shape of Pastoral Integrity* (Grand Rapids: Eerdmans, 1987), 2.
4. Peterson and Dawn, *Unnecessary Pastor,* 5.
5. Ibid., 70.

Chapter 3: The Necessity and Uniqueness of Biblical Leadership

1. Leonard Sweet, *Soul Tsunami* (Grand Rapids: Zondervan, 1999), 17.
2. L. Shannon Jung and Mary A. Agria, *Rural Congregational Studies* (Nashville: Abingdon, 1997), 77.
3. Ibid., 79.
4. Patricia M. Y. Chang, *Assessing the Clergy Supply in the Twenty-first Century* (Durham, N.C.: Duke Divinity School, 2004), 16.
5. J. Oswald Sanders, *Spiritual Leadership* (Chicago: Moody, 1980), 40.
6. Roy Oswald and Otto Kroeger, *Personality Type and Religious Leadership* (Washington, D.C.: Alban Institute, 1992).
7. Joseph Stowell, *Shepherding the Church into the Twenty-first Century* (Wheaton, Ill.: Victor, 1994), 75.
8. William Lawrence, "Distinctives of Christian Leadership," *Bibliotheca Sacra* 144, no. 575 (July 1987): 329.
9. Ibid., 321.
10. Eugene Habecker, *Rediscovering the Soul of Leadership* (Wheaton, Ill.: Victor, 1996), 112.
11. Stowell, *Shepherding the Church,* 103.
12. Warren Bennis and Burt Nanus, *Leaders* (New York: Harper and Row, 1985), 222–23.
13. George Barna, *Today's Pastors* (Ventura, Calif.: Regal, 1993), 61.
14. Robert Anderson, *The Effective Pastor* (Chicago: Moody, 1985), 97.
15. Nolan Harmon, *Ministerial Ethics and Etiquette* (Nashville: Abingdon, 1987), 47.
16. Patricia H. Virga, ed., *The NMA Handbook for Managers* (Englewood Cliffs, N.J.: Prentice Hall, 1987), 126.
17. Erwin Lutzer, *Pastor to Pastor* (Chicago: Moody, 1987), 76.
18. Barna, *Today's Pastors,* 36.
19. Ibid., 37.
20. Gerald W. Gillaspie, *The Restless Pastor* (Chicago: Moody, 1974), 15.
21. David Hansen, *The Power of Loving Your Church* (Minneapolis: Bethany, 1998), 43.

22. Ibid., 61.

Chapter 4: The Foundation of Leadership

1. See Herman A. Hoyt, "The Divine Call to the Ministry of Jesus Christ," *Grace Journal* 14, no. 1 (Winter 1973), 4.
2. William D. Lawrence, "Distinctives of Christian Leadership," *Bibliotheca Sacra* 144, no. 575 (July–Sept 1987): 322.
3. Concerning this call, Herman Hoyt points to the relationship between the efficacious call to salvation and the call to ministry, "Associated with this efficacious call to salvation the call to service is intimately related. Chronologically this may be immediate, or it may be more remotely separated. But one thing is certain, that when God saves men, he saves them for something." Hoyt goes on to point out, "But in either case it is associated with that efficacious call to salvation. And 'the gifts and calling of God are without repentance' (Romans 11:29). In the same sense in which the efficacious call of God to salvation is sure and steadfast, so also is the effective call of God to service." Hoyt, "The Divine Call to the Ministry of Jesus Christ," 5–6. For further discussion see also, Ralph G. Turnbull, ed., *Baker's Dictionary of Practical Theology* (Grand Rapids: Baker Book House, 1967), 292.
4. Patricia M. Y. Chang, *Assessing the Clergy Supply in the Twenty-First Century* (Durham, N.C.: Duke Divinity School, 2004), 2.
5. William Hendriksen, *1 Timothy*, New Testament Commentary (Grand Rapids: Baker, 1957), 127.
6. The term "temperate" has the idea of being in control of one's thought process and being clear minded. See Johannes P. Louw and Eugene Albert Nida, ed., *Greek-English Lexicon of the New Testament: Based on Semantic Domains* (1989; New York: United Bible Societies, 1996), electronic ed. of the 2nd edition.
7. Eugene H. Peterson, *Working the Angles: The Shape of Pastoral Integrity* (Grand Rapids: Eerdmans, 1987), 38.
8. Norman Shawchuck and Roger Heuser, *Leading the Congregation* (Nashville: Leading the Congregation, 1993), 173.
9. John Piper, *Brothers, We Are Not Professionals* (Nashville: Broadman and Holman, 2002), 54.
10. Ibid., 53.
11. For a discussion on the theological perplexity of prayer, see, John D. Hannah, "Prayer and the Sovereignty of God," *Bibliotheca Sacra* 136, no. 544 (October 1979): 345–54.

12. Henry Blackaby and Richard Blackaby, *Spiritual Leadership* (Nashville: Broadman and Holman, 2001), 150.
13. Ibid.

Chapter 5: The Purpose of Leadership, Part 1

1. Stephen Charnock, *The Existence and Attributes of God,* 2 vols. (Grand Rapids: Baker, 1979), 1:24.
2. Millard Erickson, *Postmodernizing the Faith* (Grand Rapids: Baker, 1998), 30.
3. Carl Henry, *Twilight of a Great Civilization* (Westchester, Ill.: Crossway, 1988), 44.
4. Glenn Wagner, *Escape from Church, Inc.* (Grand Rapids: Zondervan, 1999), 148.
5. B. F. Westcott, *Gospel of St. John* (London: John Murray, 1892), 152.

Chapter 6: The Purpose of Leadership, Part 2

1. Henry Blackaby and Richard Blackaby, *Spiritual Leadership* (Nashville: Broadman and Holman, 2001), 20.
2. Millard J. Erickson, *Christian Theology,* 3 vols. (Grand Rapids: Baker, 1985), 3:1026.
3. Ibid., 3:1028.
4. Ibid., 3:1030.
5. Peter Senge, *The Fifth Discipline: The Art and Practice of the Learning Organization* (New York: Currency Doubleday, 1994), 359.
6. Robert L. Saucy, *The Church in God's Program* (Chicago: Moody, 1972), 19.
7. See Elmer Martens, *God's Design: A Focus on Old Testament Theology* (Grand Rapids: Baker, 1981), 81–93.
8. Robin J. Trebilcock, *The Small Church at Large* (Nashville: Abingdon, 2003), 16.

Chapter 7: The Purpose of Leadership, Part 3

1. Os Guinness, "Mission and Modernity: Seven Checkpoints on Mission in the Modern World," in *Faith and Modernity*, ed. P. Sampson, V. Samuel, and C. Sugden (Oxford: Regnum Books, 1994), 352.
2. Leon Woods, *The Prophets of Israel* (Grand Rapids: Baker, 1983), 67–68.
3. Carl F. Henry, *The Christian Mindset in a Secular Society* (Portland: Multnomah, 1984), 99.

4. D. A. Carson, *Sermon on the Mount* (Grand Rapids: Baker, 1984), 30.
5. Cornelia Butler Flora, et al., *Rural Communities: Legacy and Change* (San Francisco: Westview, 1992), 61.
6. Ibid., 63.
7. Arthur Vidich and Joseph Bensman, *Small Town in Mass Society* (Princeton: Princeton University Press, 1968), 228.
8. Flora, et al., *Rural Communities,* 278.
9. Leonard Sweet, *Soul Tsunami* (Grand Rapids: Zondervan, 1999), 17.
10. Flora, et al., *Rural Communities,* 288.
11. Ibid., 289.
12. Economic Research Service, "Rural Income, Poverty, and Welfare: High-poverty Counties," Briefing Room, updated January 29, 2004, http://www.ers.usda.gov/Briefing/IncomePovertyWelfare/HighPoverty/ (accessed December 10, 2005).
13. Carolyn Rogers, "The Older Population in Twenty-first Century Rural America," *Rural America* 17, no. 3 (Fall 2002): 7.
14. Walter Kaiser, *Toward Old Testament Ethics* (Grand Rapids: Academie, 1983), 212.
15. Darius Salter, *American Evangelism* (Grand Rapids: Baker, 1996), 368.
16. Kennon L. Callahan, *Visiting in an Age of Mission* (San Francisco: Harper, 1994), 6–7.
17. Ibid., 25.
18. Salter, *American Evangelism,* 367.
19. Kevin Ruffcorn, *Rural Evangelism* (Minneapolis: Augsburg, 1994), 25.

Chapter 8: The Priority of Leadership, Part 1

1. Colin Brown, ed., *New International Dictionary of New Testament Theology,* 3 vols. (Grand Rapids: Regency, 1976), 2:102.
2. Ibid., 3:904.
3. Geoffrey W. Bromiley, *Theological Dictionary of the New Testament,* abridged in 1 vol. (Grand Rapids, Eerdmans, 1985), 1193.
4. Eugene Peterson, *Working the Angles: The Shape of Pastoral Integrity* (Grand Rapids: Eerdmans, 1987), 161–62.
5. Joseph Stowell, *Shepherding the Church into the Twenty-First Century* (Wheaton, Ill.: Victor, 1994), 129.
6. Steve R. Bierly, *How to Thrive as a Small Church Pastor* (Grand Rapids: Zondervan, 1998), 102.
7. Ibid., 101.
8. H. B. London Jr. and Neil B. Wiseman, *Pastors at Risk* (Wheaton, Ill.: Victor, 1993), 22.
9. Brown, *Dictionary of New Testament Theology,* 3:933–35.

10. See Patricia M. Y. Chang, *Assessing the Clergy Supply in the Twenty-First Century* (Durham: Duke Divinity School, 2004).
11. George Barna, *Today's Pastors* (Ventura, Calif.: Regal, 1993), 62.
12. Stowell, *Shepherding the Church,* 153.
13. David Hansen, *The Power of Loving Your Church* (Minneapolis: Bethany, 1998), 61.
14. Stowell, *Shepherding the Church,* 103.

Chapter 9: The Priority of Leadership, Part 2

1. See books dealing with cultural shifts, such as George Barna, *Boiling Point* (Ventura, Calif.: Regal, 2001); and Leonard Sweet, *Soul Tsunami* (Grand Rapids: Zondervan, 1999).
2. See James Davison Hunter, *Culture Wars* (New York: Basis, 1991).
3. Haddon Robinson, *Biblical Preaching* (Grand Rapids: Baker, 1980), 18.
4. William Willimon and Robert L. Wilson, *Preaching and Worship in the Small Church* (Nashville: Abingdon, 1980), 114.
5. See Robinson, *Biblical Preaching;* and Walter Kaiser, *Toward an Exegetical Theology* (Grand Rapids: Baker, 1981).
6. Robert Thomas, "Precision as God's Will for My Life," pamphlet (Panorama City, Calif.: The Master's Seminary, 1989).
7. Robinson, *Biblical Preaching,* 24.
8. Quoted in Robinson, *Biblical Preaching,* 12.
9. See John R. W. Stott, *Between Two Worlds* (Grand Rapids: Eerdmans, 1982).
10. See Robinson, *Biblical Preaching,* 20.
11. Os Guinness and John Seel, *No God, but God* (Chicago: Moody, 1992), 185.
12. Willimon and Wilson, *Preaching and Worship in the Small Church,* 117–18.
13. Stott, *Between Two Worlds,* 144.
14. Warren Wiersbe and David Wiersbe, *The Elements of Preaching* (Wheaton, Ill.: Tyndale, 1986), 88.

Chapter 10: The Responsibility of Leadership

1. Colin Brown, ed., *The New International Dictionary of New Testament Theology* (Grand Rapids: Zondervan, 1975), 1:191.
2. A. T. Robertson, *Studies in the Epistle of James* (Nashville: Broadman, n.d.), 189.
3. John Thiessen, *Pastoring the Smaller Church* (Grand Rapids: Zondervan, 1981), 91.

4. Kennon L. Callahan, *Visiting in an Age of Mission* (San Francisco: Harper, 1994), 6.
5. David Ray, *The Big Small Church Book* (Cleveland: Pilgrim Press, 1992), 139.
6. Douglas Walrath, *Making It Work: Effective Administration in the Small Church* (Valley Forge, N.Y.: Judson Press, 1994), 6.
7. See Glenn Daman, *Shepherding the Small Church* (Grand Rapids: Kregel, 2002).
8. Walrath, *Making It Work*, 20.
9. A. T. Robertson, *Word Pictures in the New Testament*, 6 vols. (Grand Rapids: Baker, 1931), 4:537.

Chapter 11: The Context of Leadership

1. Bill Moore, quoted in George Barna, *The Power of Vision* (Ventura, Calif.: Regal, 2003), 168.

About Village Missions

Village Missions is a Christ-centered, faith missionary fellowship ministering to the spiritual needs of mostly rural communities of North America. The purpose of Village Missions is to provide full-time, qualified, spiritual leadership—primarily to rural areas in the United States and Canada, where there exists a definite need to win and disciple people to Jesus Christ through the proclamation and demonstration of the gospel—and to continue such leadership as requested.

The Center for Leadership Development exists to strengthen and encourage small-church leadership by providing educational and ministry training for those who serve the small church.

For more information contact:

Village Missions
Center for Leadership Development
P.O. Box 197
Dallas, OR 97338
www.village-missions.com

About the Author

Glenn Daman (D.Min., Trinity Evangelical Divinity School; M.A. in New Testament Studies and M.A. in Old Testament Studies, Western Seminary) serves as director of the Center for Leadership Development, a ministry of Village Missions, and is an adjunct professor for several Bible colleges and seminaries, teaching in the discipline of small-church studies. He has served as pastor in small churches in Washington, Oregon, and Montana, and is the author of *Shepherding the Small Church,* also published by Kregel.

ALSO BY GLENN C. DAMAN

This indispensable source of advice and encouragement for the small church pastor includes several keys to effective small church ministry, including:

- understanding the cultures of the community and the church;
- laying a theological foundation;
- learning to love God and others;
- uniting the body through vision; and
- developing a mission of reaching, teaching, and recruiting.

0-8254-2449-6 • 288 pages • Paperback